Do This In Memory of Me

Do This In Memory of Me

Cat Walsh

PLAYWRIGHTS CANADA PRESS
TORONTO

For professional or amateur production rights, please contact Playwrights Canada Press.

LIBRARY AND ARCHIVES CANADA CATALOGUING IN PUBLICATION
Title: Do this in memory of me / Cat Walsh.
Names: Walsh, Cat, author.
Description: A play.
Identifiers: Canadiana (print) 2021031575X | Canadiana (ebook) 20210315776 | ISBN 9780369102782 (softcover) | ISBN 9780369102799 (PDF) | ISBN 9780369102805 (HTML)
Classification: LCC PS8645.A4695 D6 2021 | DDC C812/.6—dc23

Playwrights Canada Press operates on Mississaugas of the Credit, Wendat, Anishinaabe, Métis, and Haudenosaunee land. It always was and always will be Indigenous land.

We acknowledge the financial support of the Canada Council for the Arts, the Ontario Arts Council (OAC), Ontario Creates, and the Government of Canada for our publishing activities.

To my family,
to James,
and to weird girls everywhere.

Do This In Memory of Me was first produced by Northern Light Theatre and L'UniThéâtre from March 15 to 25, 2018, at La Cité Francophone, Edmonton, with the following cast and creative team:

Nicole St. Martin: Genevieve
Brian Dooley: Father / Father Paul
Steve Jodoin: Martin / St. Pancras

Director: Trevor Schmidt
Set and Costume Design: Trevor Schmidt
Lighting Design: Beth Dart
Original Composition and Sound Design: Darrin Hagen
Projection and Multimedia Design: Matt Schuurman
Stage Manager: Kiidra Duhault
Production Manager: Adam Tsuyoshi Turnbull
French Translation (*En mémoire de moi*): Manon Beaudoin

Ecclesiastical Pronunciation Guide

Vowels
A as in father
E (when closed in by a consonant) as in met
E (at the end of a syllable) as in thcy
I as in machine
O as in note
OO as in boot
Y is the same as i

Consonants before ae-e-oe-i-y
C = ch as in chain
CC = tch as in catchy
SC = sh as in sheep
G = soft as in gentle

Consonants in other cases
C = k as in cot
CC = kk as in accord
SC = sk as in tabasco
G = hard as in go

Characters

GENEVIEVE: Twelve years old. The only daughter in a large Catholic family.

MARTIN THERIAULT: Twelve years old. One of Genevieve's friends. Habs fan.

FATHER PAUL: A preoccupied parish priest.

GENEVIEVE'S FATHER: A man with a secret.

ST. PANCRAS OF ROME: A fourteen-year-old martyr from the fourth century. High-strung.

The action of the play takes place in late 1963 over one week in Montreal.

The atmosphere is dreamy and slightly ominous. Lights shine through stained glass windows. Music—perhaps the low solemn tone of an organ or a Gregorian chant. The Roman Rite is imminent.

From out of the shadows steps GENEVIEVE, *a girl of about twelve. She carries the processional cross. She wears a white alb and is followed by two other altar servers wearing white albs with hoods that obscure their faces. One carries the processional candle, the other carries the prayer book.*

As GENEVIEVE *plants the processional cross in its holder, one of the other servers hands her the prayer book. The two other servers turn and exit.* GENEVIEVE *waits, facing up stage.*

Beat. GENEVIEVE *looks behind her, expecting to see the priest, or at least the other servers returning.*

She is alone.

Beat.

She turns to face the audience, shifting from one foot to the other.

Pause.

Finally she opens the prayer book, frantically turning pages. She clears her throat.

In the distance, we hear bells ringing. GENEVIEVE *turns around. Silence.*

She turns back to the congregation. She makes the sign of the cross. She speaks nervously.

GENEVIEVE: In nomine Patris et Filii et Spiritus— *[In the name of the Father and the Son and the Spirit—]*

She clears her throat, begins again, more confidently.

In nomine Patris et Filii et Spiritus—

A figure in black scuttles across the stage quickly behind her, pausing to shush her. She whirls around, but the figure is gone.

—et Spiritus Sancti. Amen. *[—and the Holy Spirit. Amen.]*

Three figures in black approach in a solemn procession. On closer inspection we see that they are wearing nuns' habits. GENEVIEVE *is unaware that they are behind her, slowly creeping closer.*

Introibo ad altare Dei. *[I will go unto the altar of God.]*

She waits for the response from an altar server, but realizes she is alone and then takes on that role as well, speeding a little through the server's part:

(as the server) Ad Deum qui laetificat juventutem meam. *[To God, Who gives joy to my youth.]*

(as priest) Judica me, Deus, et discerne causam meam de gente non sancta: ab homine iniquo et doloroso erue me. *[Judge me, O God, and distinguish my cause from the unholy nation, deliver me from the unjust and deceitful man.]*

> *The nuns seize her and begin to drag her off stage.* GENEVIEVE *tries to fight them off, still saying the mass. The nuns subdue her by whipping her with rosaries, hitting her with their crucifixes.*

Hey!

Quia tu es, Deus, fortitudo mea: quare me repulisti—let go of me—et quare tristis incedo dum affligit me inimicus? *[For Thou, O God, art my strength, why hast Thou cast me off? And why do I go about in sadness, while the enemy afflicts me?]*

Let me go!

> *Her yelling grows louder and louder until she is pulled off stage completely.*

> *A long column of light spreads across the stage—a shadowy figure in a doorway.* GENEVIEVE *tumbles on stage, wearing her nightgown. She's fallen out of bed during a nightmare.*

FATHER: Genevieve? Is everything all right in here?

GENEVIEVE: I . . . yes. Just a bad dream.

FATHER: Oh. Well. Don't worry, it's just a dream.

GENEVIEVE: I know, Dad.

FATHER: So . . . there's nothing to be afraid of.

GENEVIEVE: I know.

FATHER: Get back to bed. You have school tomorrow. And make sure you're up early enough to pack lunch for your brothers.

GENEVIEVE: But, Dad—

FATHER: Who else is going to do it?

Beat.

Do you have a suggestion?

GENEVIEVE: I thought . . .

FATHER: . . . Yes?

GENEVIEVE: Well, can't they do it themselves?

FATHER: I don't want any more arguments about this—

GENEVIEVE: I'm not!

FATHER: You're going to have to help out around the house for a little while.

GENEVIEVE: I know. But . . .

FATHER: But?

GENEVIEVE: If I'm old enough to help out and make lunches . . . I mean, Luke and Phillip are older than me.

FATHER: So?

GENEVIEVE: So can't they help me? Or make their own lunches?

FATHER: Luke and Phillip have other things to worry about.

GENEVIEVE: Like what?

FATHER: Like school.

GENEVIEVE: I have school too.

FATHER: School is much harder when you're older.

GENEVIEVE: Phillip watches TV after you go to bed.

FATHER: Genevieve.

GENEVIEVE: He does! Every night!

FATHER: What did I say about tattling?

GENEVIEVE: Until really late.

FATHER: Genevieve?

GENEVIEVE: You said don't tattle.

FATHER: Be sure to include tattling in your next confession.

GENEVIEVE: I don't think Jesus cares about tattling.

FATHER: You shouldn't presume to know what He cares about. Be sure to include that in your confession too. Now get to bed, you have to get up early. And remember to pack a lunch for me too.

GENEVIEVE: Yes, Dad.

FATHER: That's settled then. Good night.

GENEVIEVE: Dad?

FATHER: What is it?

GENEVIEVE: When is Mom coming home?

FATHER: . . .

GENEVIEVE: Have you talked to her?

FATHER: Not today.

GENEVIEVE: Oh.

FATHER: I think she might call tomorrow. Now back to bed before you wake up your brothers.

GENEVIEVE: Good night.

FATHER: Good night.

> *The door closes.* GENEVIEVE *is alone in her room. She kneels and begins to pray.*

GENEVIEVE: Heavenly Father, please let me sleep well tonight because I have a test tomorrow—I'm sure you knew that already, but you have a lot going on so you might lose track of little details like that. Anyway, it's a science test. Please let me do well? Or even if I don't do well, at least let me do better than Martin Theriault. Even though my dad says that girls don't need to learn science, please, please let me do better than Martin. Thy will be done, amen.

Oh, one more thing . . . does Jesus care about tattling? I don't think he would, especially with everything else going on in the world. In fact, I'm sure there are much more important issues to deal with than me telling my dad that Phillip stays up late every night watching television, which of course you and Jesus already know about anyways.

My dad says it's not my place to assume what you or Jesus care about, but me tattling wouldn't be the same as, I don't know, killing somebody, or committing adultery, or stealing, right?

Beat.

Anyway . . . please keep my mother safe, wherever she is, and please ask her to call us soon. And bless my father and Nicholas, Paul, Robert, Luke, and Phillip. Thank you. Good night. Sleep well.

Beat.

You probably don't sleep. You're probably answering prayers from Australians right now. It's daytime there. It's always daytime somewhere, because the earth—you know all that already. Sorry. Anyway. Don't forget about the science test. And if you want to give me some divine inspiration, please feel free?

Okay. Well . . .

Oh! Remember how I was going to talk to Father Paul? Want to see something?

She goes to her book bag and pulls out a small book, which has clearly been read many times. It's the instructional booklet for altar servers.

I've been practising.

She reads aloud from the book.

"There are three kinds of bowing:

A head bow.

> *She demonstrates.*

A medium bow.

> *She demonstrates.*

A profound bow."

> *She demonstrates.*

Pretty good, right?

> *She flips through the book. She stops to read out loud, acting out the various steps as she says them.*

"Altar server one picks up the bells. Return to the front steps, genuflect, then both servers return to the corners and kneel.

At the Sanctus, ring the bell three times."

> *She picks up imaginary bells and rings them. The sound of bells is heard.*

"Make the sign of the cross with the priest at the benediction. The priest prays silently. Remain kneeling.

The priest places his hand over the host and the chalice. This is your cue to ring the bell one time."

She rings the bells again.

"Rise, genuflect, and ascend to the highest step for the consecration. Kneel down. Altar server one carries the bells with him."

Or her.

You know, I had that dream again. About the mass. And the nuns. Is it some kind of message?

Is it one of those things I'm going to have to find out for myself?

Sorry. I know, you're busy. Australians.

Lucy St. Germain says she's going to be a nun. She has it all planned out. Her grandmother is thrilled. She's insufferably pious, if you don't mind my saying so. Lucy, not her grandmother, although that kind of thing does seem to run in families. If you are talking to her, maybe ask her to tone it down a little? And I'm sure one of my brothers is going to be a priest. It doesn't even matter which one—my grandmother will be so happy.

How do I know if that's what I'm supposed to do? Or more importantly, how do I know if that's not what I'm supposed to do?

I asked my grandmother about it, and she said those who are true servants of God would hear a call.

That's it. Very mysterious. Did you call Lucy?

Will you call me?

    Distantly, in the house, the phone begins ringing.

Oh.

Is that . . . are you . . . ? I didn't mean tonight.

The phone continues to ring.

You'll wake up my father. He'll be very, very angry about me getting a phone call this late at night, no matter who it is.

Now he's up. He's going downstairs—

The phone stops ringing. GENEVIEVE *waits. Pause.*

Can you just call back later? Or just hang up. Hang up!

Pause.

FATHER *comes back upstairs. A thin shaft of light appears across the floor as he opens her bedroom door.*

FATHER: Genevieve, are you still awake?

GENEVIEVE: Who was on the phone?

Beat.

Dad?

FATHER: Go to sleep.

The door closes. GENEVIEVE *waits for a moment, then continues her prayer.*

GENEVIEVE: What did you say to him?

Pause.

Remember: better than Martin on the science test. Amen.

She goes to bed.

A flock of nuns rushes by.

The next day, in church, MARTIN *is outside the confessional with a hockey stick, practising his stickwork. He is wearing a new-looking Canadiens jersey.*

MARTIN: And he intercepts the pass . . . he's heading to the blue line . . . no one can catch him!

GENEVIEVE enters.

GENEVIEVE: Hi, Martin.

MARTIN is absorbed in his imaginary hockey game and ignores her.

MARTIN: He shoots . . . he scores! The crowd is going crazy!

MARTIN makes the sound of a roaring crowd.

GENEVIEVE: *(louder this time)* Hi, Martin.

MARTIN: They're going to have to stop the game to get everyone under control! Even the other team is cheering! They're all chanting "GO GO, THERIAULT! GO GO, THERIAULT!"

GENEVIEVE: MARTIN!

MARTIN continues to play through their conversation.

MARTIN: What?

GENEVIEVE: You'll get in trouble if Father Paul catches you.

MARTIN: No I won't.

> *Beat.*

GENEVIEVE: Pretty tough test today.

MARTIN: Did you think so?

GENEVIEVE: . . . What did you think?

MARTIN: It wasn't so bad.

GENEVIEVE: Yeah, it was pretty easy.

MARTIN: You like my jersey?

GENEVIEVE: It's nice.

MARTIN: It's an early birthday present. My dad got it for me for my birthday on Thursday.

GENEVIEVE: Happy birthday.

MARTIN: It's not my birthday.

GENEVIEVE: I know.

MARTIN: My birthday's on Thursday.

GENEVIEVE: Okay.

MARTIN: You can wish me happy birthday then.

GENEVIEVE: Where were you this afternoon?

MARTIN: Will you?

GENEVIEVE: Will I what?

MARTIN: Remember to wish me a happy birthday.

GENEVIEVE: Sure.

MARTIN: You'd better.

GENEVIEVE: How come you weren't in school?

MARTIN: There was a funeral this afternoon.

GENEVIEVE: Who?

MARTIN: Mrs. McKee. Do you know her?

GENEVIEVE: No.

MARTIN: She had cancer.

GENEVIEVE: That's sad.

MARTIN: I was excused to serve at mass.

GENEVIEVE: They let you out of school to do that?

MARTIN: All the time. Or whenever someone dies.

GENEVIEVE: Did a lot of people come?

MARTIN: What's a lot?

GENEVIEVE: I don't know.

MARTIN: It was pretty respectable, I guess. I'd be happy if that many people came to mine. Guess what we did afterward?

GENEVIEVE: Who?

MARTIN: Me and Scott. Guess what we did.

GENEVIEVE: I don't know, what?

MARTIN: We drank the leftover communion wine.

GENEVIEVE: No!

MARTIN: Don't tell anyone.

GENEVIEVE: Who am I going to tell?

MARTIN: You tell people things.

GENEVIEVE: No I don't.

MARTIN: Okay.

GENEVIEVE: Are you drunk?

MARTIN: I don't know. Maybe. Do I seem drunk?

GENEVIEVE: No.

MARTIN: Don't tell anyone.

GENEVIEVE: What's it like? Is it fun?

MARTIN: Yes. I feel kind of sick. But yes.

GENEVIEVE: Maybe you should stop running around so much.

MARTIN: Do you want to try it?

GENEVIEVE: Now?

MARTIN: Next time we're at mass. I could try and sneak some out to you afterward.

GENEVIEVE: No, thanks.

MARTIN: Do you have a Thermos?

GENEVIEVE: My dad would kill me.

MARTIN: Don't your parents ever drink wine at dinner?

GENEVIEVE: Not holy wine!

MARTIN: There's no difference.

GENEVIEVE: Martin!

MARTIN: Your dad would never find out.

GENEVIEVE: He'd find out.

MARTIN: Suit yourself.

GENEVIEVE: Why are you still hanging around here?

MARTIN: I had to talk to the father about the server schedule.

GENEVIEVE: Too many early morning masses?

MARTIN: We're going to visit my aunt next weekend. I have to find a sub. If I don't have a sub, Father Paul will call my parents. Again. What are you doing here?

GENEVIEVE: Why?

MARTIN: You're always hanging out here. It's weird.

GENEVIEVE: It's not weird. And I'm not always here.

MARTIN: You trying to become a nun or something?

GENEVIEVE: No!

MARTIN: Weird.

GENEVIEVE: I'm going to talk to Father Paul. About becoming an altar server.

> *Beat.*

MARTIN: You?

GENEVIEVE: Yes, me. Who knows, maybe I can sub for you next weekend.

MARTIN: I don't think so.

GENEVIEVE: I don't mind—

MARTIN: You can't be an altar server.

GENEVIEVE: Why not?

MARTIN: You're a girl.

GENEVIEVE: That's very observant.

MARTIN: Well, you are.

GENEVIEVE: Why can't girls be altar servers?

MARTIN: Have you ever seen a girl altar server?

GENEVIEVE: Well, no—

MARTIN: There you go.

GENEVIEVE: Someone has to be the first.

MARTIN: I don't think so. It's in the Bible.

GENEVIEVE: Girls can do anything boys can do.

MARTIN: That's definitely not true.

GENEVIEVE: A woman went into space.

MARTIN: Yeah, a Russian woman.

GENEVIEVE: So?

MARTIN: That's pretty much the same as a man.

GENEVIEVE: That's very immature.

MARTIN: You could be a nun.

GENEVIEVE: I don't want to—

MARTIN: Then you can be a teacher. Or a nurse. My mother says it opens a lot of doors for women.

GENEVIEVE: But I want to be here.

MARTIN: You could be downstairs with the Ladies' Auxiliary. Help them make sandwiches.

GENEVIEVE: I can make sandwiches already.

MARTIN: They had so many kinds of sandwiches after the funeral today. Egg salad. Tuna salad. Chicken salad. Ham salad.

GENEVIEVE: Why don't you go make sandwiches if you like them so much.

MARTIN: Why? The ladies downstairs make them for me.

GENEVIEVE: You should learn to make your own.

MARTIN: Father Paul's going to say no.

GENEVIEVE: He doesn't like me.

MARTIN: I have to go to hockey practice.

GENEVIEVE: Maybe I should play hockey too.

MARTIN: You can't play hockey.

GENEVIEVE: Why not?

MARTIN: Same reason you can't be an altar server.

GENEVIEVE: Shut up, Martin.

MARTIN: Did you just tell me to shut up in church? That's a sin.

GENEVIEVE: It's not a sin.

MARTIN: You'd better go to confession.

GENEVIEVE: Shut up. And don't tell me to go to confession.

MARTIN: Do you skate?

GENEVIEVE: I . . . No.

MARTIN: Then how are you going to play hockey?

GENEVIEVE: I could learn.

MARTIN: Uh-huh.

GENEVIEVE: You don't know anything about what I can do.

MARTIN: I know Father Paul's not going to let you up on the altar at mass.

GENEVIEVE: You're just afraid I'll be better at it than you.

MARTIN: Yeah, that must be it. Well. Good luck.

GENEVIEVE: Have fun at practice.

MARTIN: Thanks. See you tomorrow.

GENEVIEVE: Not if I see you first.

MARTIN: Good one.

MARTIN exits.

GENEVIEVE: Heavenly Father: this is it. Please, please, please let Father Paul see things my way. Amen.

Oh, also: Why were there so many test questions about the circulatory system? I didn't study that. I thought we had a deal. Amen.

I'm sorry, I know you don't make deals. But if you could just grant me this one thing, I will never ask for anything again. Deal?

Amen.

FATHER PAUL enters. He seems distracted.

FATHER PAUL: Oh, Genevieve. Good afternoon.

GENEVIEVE: Hello, Father.

FATHER PAUL: Have you seen Martin Theriault by any chance?

GENEVIEVE: He just left. He said he was going to hockey practice.

FATHER PAUL: I see.

GENEVIEVE: I was hoping to talk to you—

FATHER PAUL: Are you here for confession? You know the regular hours are—

GENEVIEVE: It's for something else, actually.

FATHER PAUL: Are you sure? When was the last time you confessed your sins?

GENEVIEVE: Last week.

FATHER PAUL: Well, no time like the present—

GENEVIEVE: I haven't really been doing anything since last week, Father. Just reading. Studying. Praying.

FATHER PAUL: All very admirable pursuits. Especially for someone of your age.

GENEVIEVE: Thank you. My teachers all say I take things very seriously for someone my age—

FATHER PAUL: It's very unusual. Martin, for example, all he wants to talk about is hockey. Hockey this, hockey that. Did you see the jersey he was wearing?

GENEVIEVE: Yes. It's just that—

FATHER PAUL: Between you and me, I wouldn't think his family would have the money to spend on little extras like that, even if it is his birthday.

GENEVIEVE: Thursday, yes. But I—

FATHER PAUL: Thursday?

GENEVIEVE: His birthday. I—

FATHER PAUL: I'll have to remember that and wish him well the next time I see him. In any case, you were here for confession?

GENEVIEVE: No, I—

FATHER PAUL: You're not here to talk about Martin? Because I think your mother would be more appropriate—

GENEVIEVE: I'm not here for confession or to talk about Martin. I want to talk to you about something else.

FATHER PAUL: All right.

GENEVIEVE: Something serious.

FATHER PAUL: Go ahead.

GENEVIEVE: Okay. Well. You see . . . Okay, I was talking to Martin—

FATHER PAUL: So this is about Martin—

GENEVIEVE: No, it's not. Only indirectly. Martin mentioned that he was trying to find a substitute to serve at mass.

FATHER PAUL: Yes. Do you think one of your brothers might be able to help us out? Of course, what a wonderful idea—

GENEVIEVE: I'm so glad you think so, because I think—

FATHER PAUL: Do you think Luke might be available?

GENEVIEVE: I don't—

FATHER PAUL: Although it's been quite a while since he served. I'm sure we can meet quickly to go over—

GENEVIEVE: Actually, Father, I have an even better idea.

FATHER PAUL: What's that?

GENEVIEVE: I thought . . . I mean, I have been thinking a lot about it . . . and reading and studying . . .

FATHER PAUL: Yes, you mentioned that—

GENEVIEVE: Well, I thought maybe . . . I could fill in for Martin. And then if that goes well, I could just be on the regular schedule after that.

FATHER PAUL: I'm sorry, I don't understand.

GENEVIEVE: I know all the responses. And I have a very steady hand— you wouldn't have to worry about me spilling the wine or knocking over a candle. And I'm quiet. I wouldn't cause any big distractions crossing from the gospel side to the epistle side—I know those are the two sides because I've been studying—and I'm light on my feet so I would never trip.

FATHER PAUL: Genevieve—

GENEVIEVE: And I'm very musical. I'd know just how much to ring the bells and when. In fact, I think I'm especially well-suited to ring the bells. I would almost say I have an affinity for it, perhaps . . . perhaps a God-given gift? And you know half the congregation are women, and I don't think you could say that men love God any more than women do—

FATHER PAUL: Genevieve—

GENEVIEVE: And if you're worried about me having my head covered, I thought I could just wear the hood up so it wouldn't cause a stir amongst the more . . . old-fashioned people in the congregation—

FATHER PAUL: What are you saying?

GENEVIEVE: I want to be an altar server, Father.

Beat.

FATHER PAUL: That's not possible.

GENEVIEVE: Why not?

FATHER PAUL: Who put an idea like this in your head?

GENEVIEVE: No one. I thought of it myself.

FATHER PAUL: One of these feminists trying to stir up trouble?

GENEVIEVE: No! It just came to me one day. Father, I want to serve.

FATHER PAUL: There are many more appropriate ways for a young woman to serve.

GENEVIEVE: What if it was God who told me to serve?

    Beat.

FATHER PAUL: Did God tell you to serve?

GENEVIEVE: We've been discussing it.

FATHER PAUL: I see. And?

GENEVIEVE: It's been a bit one-sided. So far. But theoretically I don't see why He wouldn't approve—

FATHER PAUL: He wouldn't approve because it's against His own rules.

GENEVIEVE: But Sister Marguerite says things are changing.

FATHER PAUL: Sister Marguerite! I should have known.

GENEVIEVE: But things are changing!

FATHER PAUL: Trust me, they are not changing that much.

GENEVIEVE: She says soon we'll go to mass in English.

FATHER PAUL: And that's enough change for one century.

GENEVIEVE: Don't you think it would be nicer for everyone to understand? To see the priest's face?

FATHER PAUL: The mass isn't about the priest putting on a show—it's about worshipping God. You tell Sister Marguerite that. No, don't tell her that. I'll speak to her myself.

GENEVIEVE: Doesn't God speak English?

FATHER PAUL: God speaks every language.

GENEVIEVE: Then why does He care whether or not we pray in Latin?

FATHER PAUL: It is a matter of respect. Genevieve, it's wonderful that you would want to serve the Lord in this way. But it's quite impossible.

GENEVIEVE: I still don't see why.

FATHER PAUL: It's simply not your place. Next thing you'll be asking for women to be ordained. Unless Sister Marguerite has told you to ask for that already. What exactly has she been telling you?

GENEVIEVE: I'm not asking to be ordained. I just want—

FATHER PAUL: It's right there in Corinthians. A woman may publicly pray in church, but she cannot teach or have authority over a man. Jesus chose twelve men to spread His word. If He'd wanted a woman to speak on His behalf, don't you think He would have chosen one?

Beat.

Well?

GENEVIEVE: My father said I shouldn't presume to know what Jesus wants.

FATHER PAUL: Oh—well, yes, that is correct. You shouldn't presume.

GENEVIEVE: But you can?

FATHER PAUL: It's not presumption. "The man is the head of the woman." He is originally ordained for the priesthood. For the woman is the body of the man, taken from his side and subject to him, from whom she was separated for the procreation of children. Of course, it's not really appropriate for me to speak any further to you with regards to procreation, but you get my meaning, don't you?

GENEVIEVE: Not really.

FATHER PAUL: Man was created in God's image. Woman was created from man. And is different from him. And so you have a different role in the church.

GENEVIEVE: Making sandwiches.

FATHER PAUL: Certainly the Ladies' Auxiliary is one avenue of service to the community. But there are many, many ways that young people can serve and inspire. There are plenty of saints who were your age, some even younger. St. Maria Goretti.

GENEVIEVE: Who's that?

FATHER PAUL: She's a virgin martyr.

GENEVIEVE: What does that mean?

FATHER PAUL: Ah. Well. A young man wanted to . . . that is, he was going to . . . well, to defile her, and when she refused him, he stabbed her. Even though he was her murderer, she forgave him on her death-bed. And she was only eleven.

GENEVIEVE: Hmmm.

FATHER PAUL: Or there's Agnes of Rome.

GENEVIEVE: Another virgin martyr?

FATHER PAUL: Oh yes. She was twelve. When she refused to . . . submit . . . to the prefect, he became so angry at her love of Christ that he had Agnes dragged through the streets naked and brought to a brothel.

GENEVIEVE: Oh.

FATHER PAUL: But! Her hair miraculously grew so that it covered her body. And even after that, anyone who tried to—to do anything to her was immediately struck blind.

GENEVIEVE: So she escaped?

FATHER PAUL: No, she was immediately sentenced to burn at the stake—

GENEVIEVE: Oh.

FATHER PAUL: But she wasn't burned—

GENEVIEVE: Oh?

FATHER PAUL: In the end she was beheaded.

Beat.

GENEVIEVE: I'm not sure this is very inspiring.

FATHER PAUL: Well, let's think. I'm sure we can find someone you can relate to . . . what about St. Dominic Savio?

GENEVIEVE: Virgin martyr?

FATHER PAUL: Oh no, he's a confessor.

GENEVIEVE: What's the difference?

FATHER PAUL: Martyrs die for their faith; confessors maintain their faith while suffering greatly.

GENEVIEVE: Are there women confessors?

FATHER PAUL: St. Dominic Savio died of pleurisy at fourteen.

GENEVIEVE: But—

FATHER PAUL: He was very holy. He was canonized just a few years ago.

GENEVIEVE: Won't you at least think about it?

FATHER PAUL: About what?

GENEVIEVE: Father!

FATHER PAUL: About you being an altar server? Oh, no. The Church is very clear on that point.

GENEVIEVE: But I really feel it's my place.

FATHER PAUL: I don't mean to sound cruel, but . . . the Church doesn't care about your feelings. Almost two thousand years of church doctrine will not be swayed by your feelings. You'll have to think of something else.

GENEVIEVE: Maybe I could go martyr myself.

FATHER PAUL: Martyrs are very fortunate. In the end, I mean. They are with God in Heaven and died defending Him. You should pray on your question some more.

GENEVIEVE: I was afraid you'd say that.

FATHER PAUL: Don't be too discouraged. There is a place for everyone in God's plan. It just might not be what we fallible humans think it is. Now, if you'll excuse me, I do have to try and find a substitute for Martin.

GENEVIEVE: Yes, Father.

FATHER PAUL *exits.* GENEVIEVE *kneels immediately.*

Dear Lord: thanks for all the help!

Sorry. But come on!

I don't want to tell you what to do, but could you maybe appear to Father Paul in a vision? Or leave him a note? Or . . . I'm sure you have some better ideas.

Or maybe I could perform a miracle. Just a small one, nothing too flashy. Just something that would show everyone, but particularly Father Paul, that you're on my side about this. Maybe levitation?

I'll let you decide. Thy will be done, amen.

A young man appears, looking to be about fourteen or so, dressed in something that suggests fourth century Rome. A halo would be great. He is ST. PANCRAS *of Rome.*

ST. PANCRAS: Genevieve!

GENEVIEVE *thinks God Himself has answered her.*

GENEVIEVE: . . . Lord?

ST. PANCRAS: Genevieve!

GENEVIEVE: You're here! Of course, you're everywhere, but . . . I'm going to get Father Paul. Don't go anywhere.

She is about to leave when ST. PANCRAS *speaks again, somewhat impatiently.*

ST. PANCRAS: Behind you!

She turns around and is startled to see him.

GENEVIEVE: Oh!

ST. PANCRAS: Oh yourself.

GENEVIEVE: Who are you?

ST. PANCRAS: Ha ha, very funny.

GENEVIEVE: No, who are you?

ST. PANCRAS: Isn't it obvious?

GENEVIEVE: No.

ST. PANCRAS: You don't recognize me from a stained glass window or maybe a prayer card . . . ?

GENEVIEVE: Um . . .

ST. PANCRAS: I am Pancras of Rome.

GENEVIEVE: Who?

ST. PANCRAS: Pancras of Rome. St. Pancras of Rome? The patron saint of children?

GENEVIEVE: I thought St. Nicholas was the patron saint of children.

ST. PANCRAS: There are enough children in the world to have more than one patron. But since you asked, I also look after jobs, health, cramps, false witnesses, headaches, and perjury.

GENEVIEVE: That's a lot of things.

ST. PANCRAS: Thank you.

GENEVIEVE: Are you a virgin martyr?

ST. PANCRAS: We just say "martyr."

GENEVIEVE: So you're not—

ST. PANCRAS: Well aren't you nosy? In fact, I am. But with men it's not necessary to specify. It's just implied. So how can I help you?

GENEVIEVE: I'm not sure.

ST. PANCRAS: Well you called for intercession, didn't you? I'm here to intercede.

GENEVIEVE: With Father Paul?

ST. PANCRAS: With God.

GENEVIEVE: Really?

ST. PANCRAS: Really.

GENEVIEVE: Can't I just ask Him directly?

ST. PANCRAS: Sometimes you need someone to put in a good word for you. Besides, maybe I can even help you myself.

GENEVIEVE: I . . .

ST. PANCRAS: Yes?

GENEVIEVE: It's just that . . .

ST. PANCRAS: Yes, speak up.

GENEVIEVE: I want to be an altar server.

ST. PANCRAS: And?

GENEVIEVE: Girls aren't allowed.

ST. PANCRAS: Yes. And?

GENEVIEVE: And I want to change the rule.

ST. PANCRAS: Oh. That's it?

GENEVIEVE: What do you mean, that's it?

ST. PANCRAS: Well, that's easy.

GENEVIEVE: It is?

ST. PANCRAS: You can't.

Beat.

GENEVIEVE: But you didn't even try!

ST. PANCRAS: I'm going to give you a valuable piece of advice: pick your battles.

GENEVIEVE: Just give up? What kind of advice is that?

ST. PANCRAS: Do you know how I was martyred?

GENEVIEVE: I've never even heard of you.

ST. PANCRAS: And it's so kind of you to keep reminding me. I was beheaded.

He puts his hands on his head as if he were about to remove it.

Want to see?

GENEVIEVE: No!

ST. PANCRAS: Fine. But it was because I refused to give up my faith. You know, my head, my actual head, is underneath a basilica that's named after me.

GENEVIEVE: Really.

ST. PANCRAS: Yes, really! You're not even a little impressed? I'm sure you have several basilicas named after you!

GENEVIEVE: It's not that—

ST. PANCRAS: I am very popular in Europe.

GENEVIEVE: Maybe I should talk to someone else.

ST. PANCRAS: You don't get to choose! And you don't get to change things to suit yourself.

GENEVIEVE: It's a silly rule.

ST. PANCRAS: But it's still a rule.

GENEVIEVE: I want to ring the bells. And carry the wine.

ST. PANCRAS: Can't you just—

GENEVIEVE: Don't say Ladies' Auxiliary.

ST. PANCRAS: Become a nun?

GENEVIEVE: I'm twelve.

ST. PANCRAS: I'm fourteen. And look where I am.

GENEVIEVE: I don't think you're supposed to rub it in people's faces. And it doesn't have to be a change. Just an exception.

ST. PANCRAS: You think you're worthy of an exception?

GENEVIEVE: . . . Yes.

ST. PANCRAS: Really.

GENEVIEVE: Yes.

ST. PANCRAS: Fine. I'll ask for an exception. But I can't guarantee what the answer will be.

GENEVIEVE: Thank you!

ST. PANCRAS: Exceptions are very rare.

GENEVIEVE: When will you find out?

ST. PANCRAS: I'll let you know when I hear.

GENEVIEVE: Should I wait here?

ST. PANCRAS: You don't have to wait here. I can find you anywhere.

GENEVIEVE: Really?

ST. PANCRAS: Trust me.

GENEVIEVE: I'll wait here.

ST. PANCRAS: Go home to your father and brothers. And wait for a sign.

GENEVIEVE: How will I know when—

ST. PANCRAS: It'll be a big one.

GENEVIEVE: Okay.

ST. PANCRAS: Anything else?

GENEVIEVE: Do you know anything about missing people?

ST. PANCRAS: Missing children?

GENEVIEVE: My mother.

ST. PANCRAS: Oh. Did she suffer from headaches?

GENEVIEVE: I don't think so.

ST. PANCRAS: Hmmm. You might want to try St. Anthony of Padua. He's really the one to go to about anything missing. People, objects. Are you sure she's missing?

GENEVIEVE: She hasn't been home in a week.

ST. PANCRAS: Definitely a case for St. Anthony. Pray to him. He gets results.

GENEVIEVE: Do you get results?

ST. PANCRAS: Blessings of the Lord be upon you! Go home and wait for a sign.

GENEVIEVE: But—

He is gone.

Amen.

Later, in GENEVIEVE's *bedroom. She's doing homework. She stops and looks up.*

I'm still waiting. Just so you know.

The phone rings.

Is this it?

Please let this be the sign, please let this be the sign . . . Amen.

> *The phone stops ringing.* GENEVIEVE *tries to listen to what's being said in the conversation.*

I can't hear anything. Can't you make Dad talk louder?

> FATHER *knocks on the door.*

FATHER: Genevieve?

GENEVIEVE: Yes?

FATHER: I just had a very concerning phone call.

GENEVIEVE: Oh? Who was it?

FATHER: It was Mrs. Theriault.

GENEVIEVE: Oh. What did she want?

FATHER: She wanted to know if you'd seen Martin.

GENEVIEVE: Not since this afternoon.

FATHER: At school?

GENEVIEVE: At church.

FATHER: What were you doing at church?

GENEVIEVE: I . . . went to make a confession.

FATHER: Did Martin say anything about where he was going?

GENEVIEVE: I think he was going to hockey practice. That's all he talks about. Why?

FATHER: Well, it seems that he's missing.

GENEVIEVE: Missing?

FATHER: He didn't come home tonight. The police are doing a search.

GENEVIEVE: Maybe he's at one of his friend's houses.

FATHER: They're talking to his friends this evening.

GENEVIEVE: Are the police coming here?

FATHER: I don't know. Look, I'm sure he's fine. He's probably walking in his front door right now.

GENEVIEVE: I hope so.

FATHER: It'll be all right.

GENEVIEVE: I wish Mom was here.

FATHER: Me too.

GENEVIEVE: Did you talk to her today?

FATHER: Not today. Maybe tomorrow.

GENEVIEVE: Oh.

FATHER: I'm sure we'll hear from her soon.

GENEVIEVE: Maybe we could go see her—

FATHER: Has anyone asked you? About your mother?

GENEVIEVE: No. Why?

FATHER: I just mean . . . well you know how people like to gossip, and her being away for a little while might get certain people talking. Right?

GENEVIEVE: I guess.

FATHER: It's really not anyone else's business outside of this house where she is.

GENEVIEVE: Do you know where she is?

FATHER: I'm going to call Mrs. Theriault back and tell her you saw Martin this afternoon. The police might want to talk to you, but I'll be with you if they do.

GENEVIEVE: That's exciting.

FATHER: I beg your pardon?

GENEVIEVE: I mean exciting in a sad way. I've never been to a police station before.

FATHER: They'll come here. There's no reason for you to go down there and associate with the criminal element who'd be lurking about.

GENEVIEVE: Oh. Well I hope they find Martin soon.

FATHER: I'm sure they will. Back to your studying. Oh, and I'd appreciate it if you didn't use the heel of the bread for my sandwiches.

GENEVIEVE: Sorry.

FATHER: It just doesn't sit properly. Gives it a strange weight in your hand. It's distracting. Give it to one of your brothers, they won't mind.

GENEVIEVE: Okay.

FATHER: Good night.

GENEVIEVE: Good night.

After he leaves, GENEVIEVE begins to pray.

Dear St. Pancras . . . is that the sign you were talking about? Or is it just a coincidence?

Did something happen to Martin? St. Pancras?

How will I know it's a sign if you don't tell me? You said it'd be a big one, and this is pretty big.

Okay. Dear Lord, if this is a sign, and I'm sure it isn't a sign, please make sure Martin is okay? Even if he is annoying sometimes, well most of the time, I didn't want him to . . . to be kidnapped or lost or anything. I didn't want any harm to come to him. Besides, you wouldn't harm another kid to answer my prayers . . . would you?

Is this your way of telling me there'll be a permanent position open in the server schedule?

I mean, it's conceivable that no one else would want to fill his spot, just because it seems like it's bad luck or cursed or something, like moving into a house where someone was murdered. If no one else wanted to take it because they worried whatever happened to Martin (even though nothing has happened to Martin) might happen to them . . . if they couldn't find anyone else, maybe they'd have to let me do it?

Is that what you're trying to tell me?

Or are you not trying to tell me anything? Couldn't you have sent St. Nicholas instead?

Okay. Please bring Martin back safely. And my mother. And bless my father and brothers. Amen.

> *The next day, in church.* GENEVIEVE *is sitting outside the confessional, humming.* FATHER PAUL *enters.*

Hi, Father.

FATHER PAUL: Hello, Genevieve.

GENEVIEVE: How are you?

FATHER PAUL: Well, I'm very distressed to hear about Martin, of course.

GENEVIEVE: They haven't found him yet?

FATHER PAUL: I haven't heard anything since yesterday. His poor mother.

GENEVIEVE: She must be very worried.

FATHER PAUL: We must all keep him and his family in our prayers.

GENEVIEVE: St. Anthony.

FATHER PAUL: Yes, that's right! You've been doing some research on the saints like I suggested.

GENEVIEVE: I have.

FATHER PAUL: Have you found anyone that you can relate to?

GENEVIEVE: St. Pancras of Rome?

FATHER PAUL: I knew you'd find someone! Although I must confess, I'm not familiar with him offhand—

GENEVIEVE: He was beheaded. He was fourteen.

FATHER PAUL: Well, that's wonderful! I mean that you have found a saint to inspire you.

GENEVIEVE: Yes. Father . . . have you given any more thought—

FATHER PAUL: Please, Genevieve. Let's not start this discussion again.

GENEVIEVE: I just thought you might have changed your mind.

FATHER PAUL: Why would I have changed my mind?

GENEVIEVE: Maybe you experienced something since the last time we talked.

FATHER PAUL: What do you mean?

GENEVIEVE: I don't know, maybe you had a strange dream, or a mysterious visitation . . .

FATHER PAUL: No, I haven't experienced anything like that.

GENEVIEVE: Or you had a headache that was miraculously healed—

FATHER PAUL: Genevieve—

GENEVIEVE: Or maybe you found a Bible passage you just hadn't read in a long time?

FATHER PAUL: Genevieve.

GENEVIEVE: Yes, Father?

FATHER PAUL: Do you really think our Lord in Heaven would perform some sort of miracle on your behalf? Particularly to convince me to bend the rules of His church?

GENEVIEVE: He has to perform miracles for someone.

FATHER PAUL: I think that statement shows you need to reflect further on this.

GENEVIEVE: Does God answer prayers or not?

FATHER PAUL: What kind of a question is that? Of course He answers prayers. But the answer isn't always "yes." Sometimes it's "no."

GENEVIEVE: Or "not yet"?

FATHER PAUL: Maybe instead of praying for yourself you should direct your energies to the plight of another. Have you been praying for Martin?

GENEVIEVE: Yes.

FATHER PAUL: Hopefully he'll be returned to his family soon.

GENEVIEVE: Have you found anyone to take his place in the meantime? I'm just curious.

FATHER PAUL: Not yet. But I suppose I'd better look for a longer-term replacement. I mean, just in case he needs time with his family when he comes back.

GENEVIEVE: You don't think they'll find him?

FATHER PAUL: Of course, of course I continue to hope he'll be found soon. But we must be prepared for all contingencies.

GENEVIEVE: In case God doesn't bring him back?

FATHER PAUL: Well, it's a bit more complex than that—

GENEVIEVE: How?

FATHER PAUL: Well you see . . . Perhaps we can schedule some time to have a longer discussion—

GENEVIEVE: Do you think God would do something to Martin?

FATHER PAUL: Of course not, God loves Martin—

GENEVIEVE: Does he not like Martin's parents?

FATHER PAUL: What a question! God loves all of His creation.

GENEVIEVE: Then why would He let Martin go missing? I'm sure his parents have been praying non-stop. Why aren't their prayers being answered? And if the answer is "no," shouldn't they at least get an answer? Wouldn't a terrible answer be better than no answer at all?

FATHER PAUL: Genevieve—

GENEVIEVE: I pray for all kinds of things, and I never get an answer.

FATHER PAUL: Genevieve, these are very complicated questions.

GENEVIEVE: Thank you.

FATHER PAUL: I don't have any answers about why things happen. We must have faith that God has a higher plan.

GENEVIEVE: That must be a pretty complex plan.

FATHER PAUL: Well, yes. The world is a very complex place.

    Beat.

GENEVIEVE: Do you think St. Anthony will help find Martin?

FATHER PAUL: He might. I think it's wonderful to pray to him to try.

GENEVIEVE: But do you think—

FATHER PAUL: Genevieve, just because you ask for something doesn't mean you'll get it. Now, I'm going to visit Martin's parents and see if there's anything I can do. Are you heading home?

GENEVIEVE: Soon. I'm supposed to make supper.

FATHER PAUL: That's very good of you to help your mother.

GENEVIEVE: Thank you.

FATHER PAUL: Well—

GENEVIEVE: I'm going to stay here and pray. For Martin.

FATHER PAUL: All right then. I'll see you later, I'm sure.

GENEVIEVE: Goodbye, Father.

> *FATHER PAUL exits. GENEVIEVE kneels.*

Heavenly Father—

> *We hear the sound of bells ringing from somewhere nearby.*
> *GENEVIEVE looks around but cannot determine the source.*
> *Silence.*

Heavenly Father—

> *The bells ring again.*

Hello?

> *The bells continue ringing.*

Who's there?

> *The bells stop.*

. . . Martin?

> *A hand emerges from the confessional, ringing the offertory bells.*
> *GENEVIEVE approaches.*

Martin, where have you—

> *ST. PANCRAS pops out from the confessional, startling her.*

ST. PANCRAS: Looking for these?

> *Beat.*

Well?

> *Ringing the bells.*

Cat got your tongue?

GENEVIEVE: I thought you were someone else.

ST. PANCRAS: Nope!

GENEVIEVE: I see that.

ST. PANCRAS: That's not very enthusiastic.

GENEVIEVE: Did you talk to God about my exception?

> *ST. PANCRAS rings the bells again.*

Well?

ST. PANCRAS: These are very fun. I can see why you want to—

GENEVIEVE: Did you talk to Him?

ST. PANCRAS: I'm waiting for the right time.

GENEVIEVE: When will that be?

ST. PANCRAS: I don't know. He has a lot of things on His mind.

GENEVIEVE: This is important!

ST. PANCRAS: It's always important. Centuries and centuries of important requests. No one ever asks me what I want.

GENEVIEVE: Do you still want for things in Heaven?

ST. PANCRAS: Well. No, not really, I suppose. But it would be nice to be asked.

GENEVIEVE: Well, what do you want?

ST. PANCRAS: *(thinks about it for a moment)* Nothing. But thank you just the same.

GENEVIEVE: You're welcome.

ST. PANCRAS: What did your priest say?

GENEVIEVE: What do you think?

ST. PANCRAS: Sorry.

GENEVIEVE: My friend Martin is missing.

ST. PANCRAS: Oh.

GENEVIEVE: He never came home last night.

ST. PANCRAS: Your mother and now your friend? Both of them missing?

GENEVIEVE: Yes.

ST. PANCRAS: My, my.

GENEVIEVE: "My, my" what?

ST. PANCRAS: Oh, nothing.

   Beat.

It's just quite a coincidence.

GENEVIEVE: I suppose.

ST. PANCRAS: Some people go their whole lives and never know a missing person.

GENEVIEVE: They're lucky.

ST. PANCRAS: But you know two.

GENEVIEVE: Yes.

ST. PANCRAS: And that's just in the past month.

GENEVIEVE: What are you suggesting?

ST. PANCRAS: I'm not suggesting anything. But I might feel a little . . . nervous if I knew you in everyday life.

GENEVIEVE: It's just a coincidence.

ST. PANCRAS: I might invest in a few St. Anthony medals myself.

GENEVIEVE: Are you saying I'm cursed?

ST. PANCRAS: Don't be so dramatic. You might just be bad luck. To others, I mean. It's nothing you can do anything about.

GENEVIEVE: Oh.

ST. PANCRAS motions to the confessional.

ST. PANCRAS: Shall we?

GENEVIEVE: Shall we what?

ST. PANCRAS: Let's go sit inside.

GENEVIEVE: To confess?

ST. PANCRAS: Just to sit.

Beat.

And maybe to confess.

GENEVIEVE: I don't have anything to confess.

ST. PANCRAS: You think I do?

GENEVIEVE: Well, no, but . . . Are you a priest?

ST. PANCRAS: I'm a saint.

GENEVIEVE: Yes, but—

ST. PANCRAS: I'm sure whatever you have to confess, I've heard worse. Get in there.

ST. PANCRAS and GENEVIEVE sit in the confessional. GENEVIEVE ends up on the priest's side. Through the magic of theatre, the interior of the confessional is visible.

Pause.

Well?

GENEVIEVE: I'm sorry, I really don't have—

ST. PANCRAS: WHAT DID YOU DO WITH MARTIN?

GENEVIEVE: What?

ST. PANCRAS: Ha ha ha, no, I'm just kidding. I'm sure you didn't do anything. Did you?

GENEVIEVE: No!

ST. PANCRAS: Because I can find out.

GENEVIEVE: I didn't!

ST. PANCRAS: I'm not saying you did. I'm joking. Can't you take a joke? Look, I'll go first. Listen carefully.

GENEVIEVE: I can't—

ST. PANCRAS: Just listen. Bless me, Genevieve, for I have sinned . . . well, I haven't really sinned at all, I suppose. So perhaps that's a lie. I confess to lying. Hmmm, no, it's not really a lie, more of a figure of speech. But I have been feeling a little . . . unfulfilled, I suppose. But that's not a sin either, is it?

    Beat.

Hello? Is it?

GENEVIEVE: I don't think so.

ST. PANCRAS: No, of course it isn't a sin, to feel a bit lost, to feel unappreciated.

GENEVIEVE: Why do you feel unappreciated?

ST. PANCRAS: I suppose I'm feeling a little . . . unimportant. I mean, you didn't know who I was—

GENEVIEVE: I haven't studied very many saints—

ST. PANCRAS: Your priest didn't know who I was.

GENEVIEVE: You heard that?

ST. PANCRAS: I hear a lot of things.

GENEVIEVE: He has a lot on his mind at the moment.

ST. PANCRAS: Yes, that must be it.

GENEVIEVE: I'm sure it's no reflection on you.

ST. PANCRAS: Do you know I've been dead over a hundred times longer than I was alive?

GENEVIEVE: But I thought a thousand years—

ST. PANCRAS: Are like a day, yes. And I'm not unhappy. I'm just not . . .

GENEVIEVE: Happy.

ST. PANCRAS: Nothing changes for me. No offence, but you're all a lot alike. Your problems are a lot alike.

GENEVIEVE: I see.

ST. PANCRAS: It's not your fault. There are a lot of things that people can't figure out, no matter how much time you give them.

GENEVIEVE: What am I supposed to do?

ST. PANCRAS: If you're unhappy you can change something. So change something. While you still can.

GENEVIEVE: No one listens to me.

ST. PANCRAS: Maybe you're not asking the right question.

GENEVIEVE: Maybe.

ST. PANCRAS: Do you forgive me?

GENEVIEVE: For what?

ST. PANCRAS: For my confession.

GENEVIEVE: What is there to forgive? You're unhappy. Or—not happy. That's not a sin. Is it?

ST. PANCRAS: You'd be surprised.

Coughing is heard off stage, followed by approaching footsteps.

GENEVIEVE: Who's that? Is it Father Paul?

ST. PANCRAS: Wait here. I'll go see.

GENEVIEVE: No, don't leave me here—

ST. PANCRAS: We haven't finished confessing. Just wait, I'll be right back.

GENEVIEVE: But—

> *Before she can protest further,* ST. PANCRAS *exits the confessional, looks in the direction of the approaching footsteps, then exits in the opposite direction.*

St. Pancras?

> FATHER *enters and steps into the other side of the confessional.*

Hello?

FATHER: Father Paul?

GENEVIEVE: Oh.

> *She tries to deepen her voice.*

Oh . . . ahem. Ahem.

FATHER: Bless me, Father, for I have sinned. It has been one month since my last confession.

I'm not sure how to begin.

> *Pause.* GENEVIEVE *begins to try and slowly exit the confessional.*

Father, it's about my wife.

> GENEVIEVE *freezes. Pause.*

Father Paul?

GENEVIEVE: *(in her best* FATHER PAUL *voice)* Yes, go ahead. My . . . son.

FATHER: I suppose you've noticed that Marie hasn't been at mass for the last couple of weeks. And I know I told you that she was under the weather, but it isn't true. And I'm sorry I lied, but I don't know what else to say.

Marie is gone. I don't even know where she is. I thought once she thought about things . . . but it's been almost three weeks, and you'd think she would have cooled off by now . . .

I came home late from work one night, not much later than usual. And the kids were downstairs watching TV and they said they'd already eaten, which was a bit strange, usually they wait and we eat together as a family. And I asked them where their mother was and Genevieve told me she was taking a bath. And when I went upstairs, Marie was just lying on the bed in the dark. She didn't even move when I turned on the light.

She was crying.

So of course I asked her what was wrong and she said, "I can't do this anymore."

And I asked her what she was talking about and she said she didn't love me anymore and hadn't for a long time. And I told her, "Marie, I'm your husband, of course you love me. What do you mean?"

And she said maybe she'd never loved me, that she'd only married me because she was pregnant with Nicholas, and she kept saying it louder and louder, "I never loved you, I never loved you, I never loved you"— and I tried to calm her down, but she was yelling and hitting at me with her fists and . . .

And so I slapped her. Just once. She wasn't thinking straight, yelling loud enough for the neighbours to hear.

And then neither of us said anything and I could feel my hand— It was tingling from the slap, and I just kept looking at my hand and she kept staring at me.

And I said, "Why don't you go to bed. We can talk about this tomorrow." And she said that was probably a good idea and she turned out the light and I went downstairs and slept on the couch.

And the next morning she was gone.

She didn't even write a note. I mean, don't you think that after nearly twenty years I deserve a note?

I thought about calling her sister or her parents to see if she was staying with one of them, but what if they didn't know either? Even if she was there, I wasn't sure they'd tell me. And of course who knows what she would have said about me.

And I've started to wonder if Marie might have done something . . . something drastic, not that I think I'd be important enough to commit such a sin over, but if she was so unhappy as to leave her family . . .

I catch myself thinking that in some way it would be—not better—but easier if she were dead, not that I want that, but there would be a finality to it. Isn't that terrible? That it's easier to think she took her own life than to . . .

Why would God allow her to be so unhappy? Or allow her to leave the children without their mother? And why wouldn't she say goodbye to them? What am I supposed to tell them? And Genevieve, she's getting to the age when she should have her mother to talk to.

What if she doesn't come back?

Do you think she's run off with another man?

Tell me what to do, Father. Please. Tell me how to bring her back. Or how to go on without—

> *He begins to break down.*

Please.

I'm so alone, Father.

> *GENEVIEVE wants to say something, but then thinks better of it. She slips out of the confessional and runs off stage.*

Father?

> *Later. GENEVIEVE's bedroom. GENEVIEVE is praying.*

GENEVIEVE: Heavenly Father.

Was there something you were planning to tell me?

What am I supposed to do? Do I tell him I know? Or relay the message to Father Paul?

Is this a test?

> *There is a knock on the closet door.*

> *Pause.*

> *More knocking. GENEVIEVE walks over to the closet.*

Hello?

She opens the door. ST. PANCRAS *steps out of the closet.*

ST. PANCRAS: Anyone home?

GENEVIEVE: I'm not talking to you.

ST. PANCRAS: Why not?

GENEVIEVE: How could you just leave me there?

ST. PANCRAS: You didn't have to stay.

GENEVIEVE: I couldn't exactly leave.

ST. PANCRAS: Of course you could have. But you didn't.

GENEVIEVE: Because I couldn't.

ST. PANCRAS: You chose not to.

GENEVIEVE: He was crying. CRYING.

ST. PANCRAS: Yes.

GENEVIEVE: Have you ever seen your father cry?

ST. PANCRAS: No, I don't think so.

GENEVIEVE: It's terrible. It's the worst thing I've ever heard. Did you know he was coming?

ST. PANCRAS: No.

GENEVIEVE: No?

ST. PANCRAS: Maybe.

GENEVIEVE: Maybe? I thought your job was to help me!

ST. PANCRAS: First of all, it's not an obligation—

GENEVIEVE: That was the opposite of helpful!

ST. PANCRAS: And I am helping you.

GENEVIEVE: How?

ST. PANCRAS: What did he say?

GENEVIEVE: You know what he said!

ST. PANCRAS: How would I know?

GENEVIEVE: Oh, please.

ST. PANCRAS: Maybe I was helping someone else. Someone who shows a little more gratitude.

GENEVIEVE: You're lying.

ST. PANCRAS: You think you're the only one who calls on me?

GENEVIEVE: I didn't call on you!

ST. PANCRAS: Yes, you keep reminding me!

GENEVIEVE: I'll bet you haven't even asked God about my problem.

ST. PANCRAS: Problem? You think you have a problem?

GENEVIEVE: Yes!

ST. PANCRAS: You know what a problem is? DECAPITATION!

GENEVIEVE: I can't help that. And besides, you're a saint.

ST. PANCRAS: So?

GENEVIEVE: Maybe you should forgive your beheaders.

ST. PANCRAS: You think you're pretty smart, don't you? Maybe you should try and solve everyone's problems. See how easy it is.

GENEVIEVE: At least I'd try to solve them!

ST. PANCRAS: Oh, all hail St. Genevieve! I can't wait to hear all your miraculous solutions.

GENEVIEVE: I think I'd be good at it. I'm a good listener. I like things to be fair.

ST. PANCRAS: Sure, that's all it takes. You'll be a fantastic success. Just remember, there are a lot more saints than there used to be. Not like it was in the fourth century. There's a bit more competition. It's all about the new, modern saints now.

GENEVIEVE: Are you saying God has favourites?

ST. PANCRAS: I don't really think I should answer that.

GENEVIEVE: How is that fair?

ST. PANCRAS: Have you really never thought about why some people's prayers are answered and some aren't?

GENEVIEVE: Father Paul says everything is unfolding according to God's plan.

ST. PANCRAS snorts.

What does that mean?

ST. PANCRAS: Nothing. Father Paul is right.

GENEVIEVE: Maybe I should talk to a more modern saint.

ST. PANCRAS: What?

GENEVIEVE: Like you said, things have really changed since the fourth century—

ST. PANCRAS: I see.

GENEVIEVE: Don't be hurt!

ST. PANCRAS: Hurt? Why would I be hurt to be forgotten—

GENEVIEVE: No—

ST. PANCRAS: Rejected—

GENEVIEVE: Pancras!

ST. PANCRAS: Ignored? Why would that hurt me? I assure you, I feel nothing but eternal and constant joy.

GENEVIEVE: You don't seem very joyful.

ST. PANCRAS: What do you know about it?

GENEVIEVE: I'm sorry, I shouldn't have asked for another saint.

ST. PANCRAS: I can understand why you would. I'm out of touch with the world.

GENEVIEVE: Just forget I said anything.

ST. PANCRAS: They think, "You're young, you should take care of the children's requests." But what do I know about what children want now? I understand they're changing the mass to the vernacular—

GENEVIEVE: I think that could be good—

ST. PANCRAS: In my day it wasn't so complicated. You professed your faith, you got beheaded, but it was a much more direct relationship. Before all these extra rules. I can hardly keep up.

GENEVIEVE: Everything's changing.

ST. PANCRAS: Tell me about it.

GENEVIEVE: It's a little scary.

ST. PANCRAS: Genevieve . . .

GENEVIEVE: Yes?

ST. PANCRAS: About your request . . .

GENEVIEVE: What is it now?

ST. PANCRAS: Look. Right now in Trois-Rivières a mother is praying her heart out that her son won't lose his leg after being in a car accident.

GENEVIEVE: And will God save his leg?

ST. PANCRAS: No.

GENEVIEVE: But—

ST. PANCRAS: Think of all those children with polio a few years ago. You think no one was praying for them?

GENEVIEVE: What are you saying?

ST. PANCRAS: If those prayers aren't answered, why would He change the rules for you?

GENEVIEVE: You haven't even asked—

ST. PANCRAS: They were in iron lungs, Genevieve. Iron lungs.

GENEVIEVE: So it's part of the plan that some kid loses his leg and only boys ever get to be altar servers?

ST. PANCRAS: I'm not really privy to the details.

GENEVIEVE: Why would God's plan be to hurt kids?

ST. PANCRAS: God loves all his children. But loving you doesn't mean giving you everything you want. Sometimes you learn more about yourself when you struggle and fail.

GENEVIEVE: Well, that's dumb.

ST. PANCRAS: I'll pass along your feedback.

GENEVIEVE: Oh, no, don't—

ST. PANCRAS: Just kidding.

GENEVIEVE: Maybe I should . . .

ST. PANCRAS: Yes?

GENEVIEVE: I mean, I guess I could . . .

ST. PANCRAS: Just say it, I'm not a mind reader! Well I am, but it's rude to do it.

GENEVIEVE: Maybe I could just talk to St. Nicholas?

ST. PANCRAS: St. Nicholas? Of course, that's who everyone wants to talk to. I'm so sorry I haven't brought toys to everyone at Christmas. I've been a little busy BEING A CHRISTIAN MARTYR!

GENEVIEVE: I didn't mean to hurt your feelings.

ST. PANCRAS: I'm not hurt.

GENEVIEVE: Yes you are.

ST. PANCRAS: I don't want to talk about it.

　　He walks into her closet.

GENEVIEVE: Wait a second—

ST. PANCRAS: If you want me to leave, I'll just leave.

GENEVIEVE: I don't want you to—

ST. PANCRAS: Maybe someone better will show up to help you.

GENEVIEVE: Can we just talk about this?

ST. PANCRAS: Don't try and stop me!

> *He closes the door.* GENEVIEVE *runs after him, trying to open the door, but she can't. It seems to be sealed shut somehow.*

GENEVIEVE: St. Pancras? Get out of there!

> *The door suddenly opens and* GENEVIEVE *is flung backward. A golden, almost heavenly light shines out of the closet door.*

St. Pancras?

> *An ominous rumbling sound is heard, like a metal anchor scraping against the side of a ship, or like some elder god being summoned from the Stygian depths.*

. . . Lord?

> MARTIN *appears wearing his Habs jersey. He's a little bit wet and bedraggled, perhaps trailing some aquatic plants or garbage behind him, caught on his shoe. He doesn't look well. The glowing and rumbling from the closet stops.*

Martin?

MARTIN: Genevieve? What are you doing here?

GENEVIEVE: This is my room.

MARTIN: Oh.

GENEVIEVE: Where's St. Pancras?

MARTIN: Who?

GENEVIEVE: Are you all right?

MARTIN: Yes. No. I don't know.

GENEVIEVE: Where have you been?

MARTIN: I fell through the ice. I thought it was solid, but—

GENEVIEVE: What happened to your nose?

MARTIN: Ducks.

GENEVIEVE: Oh.

MARTIN: Yeah, "Oh." This is your fault.

GENEVIEVE: What? How?

MARTIN: You made Him notice me.

GENEVIEVE: What are you talking about?

MARTIN: You prayed about me.

GENEVIEVE: No I didn't.

MARTIN: You did something. I should have known you weren't just weird. You're WEIRD. Anyway, someone was listening to you and I fell through the ice, and now I'm up here.

GENEVIEVE: In Heaven?

MARTIN: I don't know exactly. Up here with all the dogs they sent to space.

GENEVIEVE: What are you talking about?

MARTIN: All the test dogs. And monkeys.

GENEVIEVE: Why would they send dogs to space?

MARTIN: To see if it was safe for people.

GENEVIEVE: How did they tell the dogs what to do?

MARTIN: What do you mean?

GENEVIEVE: How did the dogs know how to fly a spaceship?

MARTIN: They didn't. They do it all from the ground.

GENEVIEVE: Oh.

MARTIN: Did you listen to last night's game?

GENEVIEVE: What about the people?

MARTIN: What?

GENEVIEVE: They sent people to space. What about them?

MARTIN: I don't know where the people go.

GENEVIEVE: They come back home, don't they?

MARTIN: I don't know. I guess.

GENEVIEVE: Have you seen any people?

MARTIN: No.

GENEVIEVE: Well, there you go. How'd you end up in dog Heaven?

MARTIN: What makes you think this is Heaven?

GENEVIEVE: You think you're in Hell?

MARTIN: I don't know.

GENEVIEVE: Dog Hell? Martin, what did you do that was so bad?

MARTIN: Maybe I'm in purgatory.

GENEVIEVE: Dog purgatory?

MARTIN: Regular purgatory.

GENEVIEVE: Do you see any unbaptized babies?

MARTIN: That's limbo. And how would I know if they were baptized?

GENEVIEVE: Wouldn't baptized ones have halos?

MARTIN: I don't see any babies.

GENEVIEVE: Look for babies without halos.

MARTIN: I don't think I'm anywhere.

GENEVIEVE: Maybe you're a figment of my imagination.

MARTIN: Ugh. That's all I need.

GENEVIEVE: You don't have to be rude. For your information, I imagine lots of fascinating things. I have a very active imagination.

MARTIN: I don't care. Stop thinking about me!

GENEVIEVE: I'm not!

MARTIN: Then why am I still here?

GENEVIEVE: How should I know? Don't sulk. Do you want to know what you're missing in school?

MARTIN: Who cares about that?

GENEVIEVE: I'm just making conversation.

MARTIN: Do you think I'm going to need algebra up here? Or history?

GENEVIEVE: So you've been there two whole days and you're already an expert on what you're going to need for eternity?

MARTIN: I don't need algebra.

GENEVIEVE: Oh! It's Thursday!

MARTIN: So?

GENEVIEVE: So happy birthday!

MARTIN: What? Oh.

GENEVIEVE: I'll bet you thought I wouldn't remember.

MARTIN: I guess I forgot.

GENEVIEVE: Well. Happy birthday.

MARTIN: It doesn't seem as important somehow.

GENEVIEVE: Good thing you got your present early.

MARTIN: What present?

GENEVIEVE: Your jersey. Remember?

MARTIN: No.

GENEVIEVE: Look down.

> *He does.*

You were so excited about it the last time I saw you. I guess you thought it would bring you better luck.

MARTIN: What day did you say it was?

GENEVIEVE: Thursday. Maybe you should write this stuff down.

> *Pause.*

So . . . do you have any powers?

MARTIN: . . .

GENEVIEVE: Like, can you move things? Or talk to other dead people? Or travel in time?

MARTIN: So far all I can do is talk to you.

GENEVIEVE: Maybe you have a celestial message for me.

MARTIN: I do: piss off.

GENEVIEVE: Go haunt someone else!

MARTIN: I'm not a ghost!

GENEVIEVE: Shut up!

MARTIN: You shut up! And stop thinking about me!

GENEVIEVE: I wish those dogs were here instead of you.

MARTIN: So do I!

> *Pause. GENEVIEVE opens a book and starts reading. MARTIN grows more impatient.*

What are you doing now?

> *She ignores him.*

Can't you at least turn on the radio or something? Maybe there's a game on.

> *She ignores him.*

WHY AM I HERE?

> *She ignores him and begins to hum softly.*

Can you imagine me a comic book or something?

GENEVIEVE: I'm sorry. I was asked to stop thinking about you.

MARTIN: But you're still doing it.

GENEVIEVE: I'm not doing anything. You know, they haven't found you yet.

MARTIN: Oh.

GENEVIEVE: Maybe you need to be buried. To find your eternal rest.

MARTIN: I don't know if I want eternal anything. That seems like a long time.

GENEVIEVE: Well, go appear to a policeman and guide him to your body.

MARTIN: If I could, I would.

GENEVIEVE: Maybe there's something you left unfinished?

MARTIN: I left everything unfinished.

Pause.

GENEVIEVE: What's it like to be missing?

MARTIN: What do you mean, what's it like? I didn't mean to be missing.

GENEVIEVE: My mother is missing, too.

MARTIN: Oh.

GENEVIEVE: I'm not supposed to know. But I overheard my dad at church—

MARTIN: Still spending a lot of time at church, huh?

GENEVIEVE: It's a long story.

MARTIN: Not interested.

GENEVIEVE: I think she's gone on some kind of trip.

MARTIN: Like a vacation?

GENEVIEVE: Maybe.

MARTIN: Lucky.

GENEVIEVE: My dad's pretty upset about it.

MARTIN: I'm sure he'll find her.

GENEVIEVE: I don't think she wants him to. I think she means to be missing.

MARTIN: Oh.

GENEVIEVE: You haven't seen her, have you?

MARTIN: Sorry.

GENEVIEVE: That's good, I guess. No offence. Are you sure you can't think of anything you left unfinished?

MARTIN: I guess the visit to my aunt. And I was working on a science project. I don't really need to finish that now.

GENEVIEVE: Do you want me to tell your parents anything? A message?

MARTIN: That would be weird.

GENEVIEVE: I would.

MARTIN: That's okay.

GENEVIEVE: I could finish your science project.

MARTIN: Why?

GENEVIEVE: I guess it doesn't matter. Maybe you're supposed to help me.

MARTIN: Maybe you're supposed to help me.

GENEVIEVE: I'm only twelve. I can't do anything.

MARTIN: I guess I'm always going to be twelve.

GENEVIEVE: Sorry.

MARTIN: Maybe Father Paul will let you replace me after all.

GENEVIEVE: I don't think so.

MARTIN: Tell him I told you it was okay.

GENEVIEVE: That'll convince him.

MARTIN: You never know.

GENEVIEVE: Yes.

> *Beat.*

What was it like?

MARTIN: What?

GENEVIEVE: When you died.

MARTIN: I don't remember. I fell through the ice. And then nothing. And then I lay there for a long time. Then the ducks came.

GENEVIEVE: Oh.

MARTIN: The ducks were the worst part.

GENEVIEVE: Did it hurt?

MARTIN: No. That was what was so bad about it.

GENEVIEVE: Maybe they'll find you soon.

MARTIN: It's almost winter. If the ice stays . . . maybe not till spring. Maybe not ever.

GENEVIEVE: That's not a good attitude—

MARTIN: But by spring there'll be even more ducks. And geese. Fish. There won't be anything left by summer.

GENEVIEVE: They'll find you before then.

MARTIN: Everyone else will be in junior high and I'll be in the river.

GENEVIEVE: They'll find you.

> *FATHER is approaching from off stage.*

FATHER: Genevieve? Are you upstairs?

MARTIN: Who's that?

GENEVIEVE: My dad. I'll be in so much trouble if he catches you here.

FATHER: Genevieve?

GENEVIEVE: Yes, just a second!

MARTIN: What makes you think he'll be able to see me?

GENEVIEVE: What if he can?

MARTIN: What if he can't?

GENEVIEVE: Martin, just . . . just wait in the closet.

MARTIN: I don't want to. It's dark.

There's a knock on the bedroom door.

FATHER: Genevieve?

GENEVIEVE: Just for a minute. Please. I'll bring you a sandwich. Whatever you want.

MARTIN: I'm not really hungry.

GENEVIEVE: Just get in!

She shoves MARTIN into the closet and closes the door just as FATHER enters the room.

FATHER: Is everything okay up here?

GENEVIEVE: Yes, fine. Why?

FATHER: I thought I heard you talking to someone.

GENEVIEVE: I'm just . . . memorizing something for school.

FATHER: I see.

GENEVIEVE: Did you . . . did you need help with something?

FATHER: No, I just wanted to see how you were.

GENEVIEVE: I'm fine.

FATHER: And I— I appreciate everything you've been doing to pitch in around the house. And I know your brothers do too.

GENEVIEVE: Thank you.

Pause.

Was there . . . was there something else you wanted to talk to me about?

FATHER: No, I don't think so.

GENEVIEVE: Are you sure?

FATHER: What are you talking about?

GENEVIEVE: I just thought . . . I mean, I have a feeling you might have something to tell me.

FATHER: No.

GENEVIEVE: Oh.

Pause.

FATHER: Well. I'll let you get back to your homework.

GENEVIEVE: Have you thought about calling Grandma?

FATHER: What?

GENEVIEVE: Maybe she's talked to Mom.

FATHER: Genevieve—

GENEVIEVE: I could call her if you want. If . . . if you're too busy with work or something.

FATHER: Maybe I'll call her from the office tomorrow—

GENEVIEVE: Don't you think Mom would want to talk to me? Even if she doesn't want to talk to you?

FATHER: Why wouldn't she want to talk to me?

GENEVIEVE: I didn't mean—

FATHER: I'm sure she wants to talk to all of us.

GENEVIEVE: Where is she?

FATHER: I don't know.

GENEVIEVE: Well you should!

FATHER: . . .

GENEVIEVE: I'm sorry. But you should.

FATHER: You're right.

GENEVIEVE: I know.

Pause.

FATHER: Have you heard anything else about your friend? Martin?

GENEVIEVE: . . . No.

FATHER: That's too bad.

GENEVIEVE: Yes.

FATHER: Well. Hopefully he'll be home soon.

GENEVIEVE: I don't think he's coming home.

FATHER: Why do you say that?

GENEVIEVE: I think something must have happened to him.

FATHER: Do you know something—

GENEVIEVE: It's just a feeling I have.

FATHER: Well. I . . . Well, I'm going to see what your brothers are up to.

GENEVIEVE: Okay.

FATHER: Let me know if you need any help. With your homework.

GENEVIEVE: I will.

> *Beat.* FATHER *exits.*

> GENEVIEVE *goes to the closet and opens the door.*

Martin, thank you for—

> *The closet is empty.*

Oh.

St. Pancras?

> *Beat.*

> *She kneels.*

Dear Lord . . . Dear Lord . . . Never mind.

> *She goes back to her homework. She picks up her book and a folded piece of paper falls out. She opens it.*

"Meet me at the church tomorrow afternoon."

> *She turns it over. There's something written on the other side as well.*

"Prepare to confess."

> *She looks up. She folds the note up and tucks it under her pillow.*

Thank you.

> *The next day.* GENEVIEVE *arrives at the church.*

> *A sister hurries by. We can't see her face.* GENEVIEVE *looks nervous.*

. . . Hello, Sister.

> *The sister does not acknowledge her and rushes off stage.*

Hello?

She is alone.

That's a little rude.

Another sister enters and hurries by, not acknowledging her.

Sister? Excuse me, Sister—

The sister exits.

Couldn't she see me?

She pokes herself, pinches herself on the arm.

Seems real enough.

She looks around.

St. Pancras?

A dog barks in the distance. It sounds distorted, perhaps as if it's being transmitted a great distance.

Martin?

The dog barks, faintly. From beneath the door to the confessional comes an eerie glow. GENEVIEVE *approaches the confessional slowly. Radio static, beeping sounds. She opens the door to the confessional and steps inside.*

Through the magic of theatre, the confessional and the church fall away. We're in space, the confessional a tiny one-person space capsule. We hear the beeping of a satellite, static, unintelligible dialogue on the radio.

Oh my.

> *The barking grows louder.*

Hello?

> MARTIN *appears on the other side of the stage, walking backward, looking around at the stars. He carries a small round space capsule: glass and metal. The capsule is broken in half, wires hanging out the sides. His face is now looking somewhat worse for wear.*

> *He does not see* GENEVIEVE. *The barking fades, growing farther away.*

MARTIN: *(whistling, as if calling a dog)* Here, boy! Come on! Here, boy!

> *He turns and notices* GENEVIEVE.

Oh.

What are you doing here?

GENEVIEVE: I don't know.

MARTIN: Were you ever going to say something?

GENEVIEVE: *(the capsule)* What's that?

MARTIN: It's a spaceship.

GENEVIEVE: Really?

MARTIN: It's broken.

GENEVIEVE: It's so small.

MARTIN: Have you seen the dog?

GENEVIEVE: What dog?

MARTIN: There's supposed to be a dog in here.

GENEVIEVE: Maybe he got out.

MARTIN: I can hear him, but I can't find him. Can you hear him?

GENEVIEVE: Did that happen often?

MARTIN: What?

GENEVIEVE: Did the dogs escape into space very often?

MARTIN: No. Mostly they just died.

GENEVIEVE: No!

MARTIN: Yes.

GENEVIEVE: That's terrible!

MARTIN: Lots of them. My dad told me.

> *Beat.*

GENEVIEVE: . . . Did they give them a funeral?

MARTIN: Do they usually give dogs funerals?

GENEVIEVE: They weren't just dogs. They were . . . scientists.

MARTIN: I think they just burned up. On their way back.

GENEVIEVE: On purpose?

MARTIN: No, dummy. They just didn't build very good rockets.

GENEVIEVE: *(referring to broken capsule)* Obviously.

MARTIN: Or it didn't matter to them if the dogs came back.

GENEVIEVE: So there was nothing left at all?

MARTIN: I guess not.

   Pause.

Are they going to give me a funeral?

GENEVIEVE: . . .

MARTIN: Are they?

GENEVIEVE: I think your parents are still hoping you'll come back.

MARTIN: So they haven't found . . .

GENEVIEVE: Not yet.

MARTIN: Oh.

GENEVIEVE: I'm sorry.

MARTIN: Have you talked to your mother?

GENEVIEVE: No. I guess you haven't seen her?

MARTIN: Sorry.

GENEVIEVE: Maybe if you look down, you'll see where she is.

MARTIN: I doubt it.

GENEVIEVE: Could you try?

MARTIN looks down.

MARTIN: Everyone looks so small, I can barely tell the difference anyways. I—huh.

GENEVIEVE: What?

MARTIN: I can't even see my house anymore. I used to be able to see my—

GENEVIEVE: Martin, can you just focus?

MARTIN: On what? She could be anywhere.

GENEVIEVE: I know.

MARTIN: Why don't you look down, then.

GENEVIEVE looks down.

GENEVIEVE: I can't see anything.

MARTIN: Oh, come on, just look there. Right there.

GENEVIEVE: There's nothing.

MARTIN: Not even dots? Everyone looks like tiny little dots.

GENEVIEVE: No.

MARTIN: Weird.

> *Beat.*

GENEVIEVE: Did you figure out what you're supposed to do?

MARTIN: No.

> *He puts the pieces of space capsule down.*

These probably aren't much good now.

I shouldn't have taken that communion wine.

GENEVIEVE: I'm sure that's not why—

MARTIN: What else could it be?

GENEVIEVE: Scott drank it too. Nothing's happened to him.

MARTIN: Not yet.

GENEVIEVE: I suppose.

MARTIN: There's no way of knowing when.

GENEVIEVE: What do you think will happen to him?

MARTIN: Who knows. Maybe something even worse.

GENEVIEVE: What could be worse?

MARTIN: I'm sure there's something. Maybe God's saving up.

GENEVIEVE: Saving up for what?

MARTIN: Something.

GENEVIEVE: It doesn't work that way.

MARTIN: Oh, I forgot, you know how everything works.

GENEVIEVE: No I don't.

MARTIN: Okay.

Beat.

GENEVIEVE: This isn't like I thought it would be.

MARTIN: What'd you expect? Angels?

GENEVIEVE: No.

MARTIN: It's space, not Heaven.

GENEVIEVE: I know that.

MARTIN: We're in space.

GENEVIEVE: I know. It's amazing.

MARTIN: It just goes on and on and on—

GENEVIEVE: I can see that.

MARTIN: We're the only ones up here.

GENEVIEVE: How do you know?

MARTIN: Trust me.

GENEVIEVE: Maybe it's higher up.

MARTIN: What?

GENEVIEVE: Heaven.

MARTIN: Maybe.

> *The radio crackles to life. Over the sounds of the beeps, boops, and chatter of mission control, the sound of ducks. Getting closer.*

I should go.

> *The sound from the radio grows louder, more insistent—unintelligible voices speaking.*

They're calling you.

GENEVIEVE: I can't understand what they're saying.

MARTIN: They're calling you back.

GENEVIEVE: How do you know?

MARTIN: What goes up must come down.

GENEVIEVE: What?

MARTIN: Good luck. *(calling the dog)* Here, boy! Here, boy!

> MARTIN *picks up the space capsule pieces and exits, still whistling for the dog.*

GENEVIEVE: Martin! Wait!

Lights and sound shift—the scary roar and glow of atmospheric re-entry intensifies until the lights and sound both snap out abruptly. The sudden silence is a little startling. We're in the re-entry blackout. A pin spot focuses on GENEVIEVE, *still in the space confessional.*

Heavenly Father:

I have questions.

Are you punishing Martin for drinking the communion wine? It seems like such a little thing. I mean in the grand scheme of things. Why would he be punished so harshly?

I'll bet if he could do it all over again, he wouldn't touch the wine. I know he wouldn't.

And is Scott next? As his accomplice? Or is his punishment the knowledge that at any time something terrible could happen to him for drinking the wine, just like it did to Martin? Just a kind of dread that he feels for his whole life? So that when something does finally happen to him it'll be a relief not to be waiting for it anymore?

Why don't you answer?

Is it because I ask for too many things for myself?

Okay, please bring Martin back to his family, in whatever state that he's in, even if it's . . . not very nice.

And please bring my mother back to our family, in whatever state she's in, even if it's not very nice.

I know that's still asking for something for me.

Please.

Are you listening?

>*Sound and lights shift as we leave the re-entry blackout—the roar and glow return.* GENEVIEVE *has to shout to be heard.*

Can you hear me?

>*Sound and lights go out.*

>*A song in the darkness. A cappella, in Latin—"Magnificat." It is beautiful.*

>*Lights up on* ST. PANCRAS *singing in the empty church. He's wearing a dog mask. The confessional is now just a confessional.* ST. PANCRAS *can't see very well through the mask and doesn't realize* GENEVIEVE *isn't there.*

ST. PANCRAS: What do you think?

Well?

>*He takes off the mask and sees he's alone.*

Oh.

>*He looks at the confessional.*

Genevieve?

>*Silence.*

I know you're in there.

Silence.

I can wait all day.

Beat.

GENEVIEVE: I'm not coming out.

ST. PANCRAS: Why not?

GENEVIEVE: I'm just not.

ST. PANCRAS: Well you can't stay in there.

GENEVIEVE: Why not?

ST. PANCRAS: It's depressing. Besides, I have something to show you.

GENEVIEVE: No thanks.

ST. PANCRAS: But it's fun!

GENEVIEVE: No.

ST. PANCRAS: All right.

He puts on the mask and starts to tiptoe over to the confessional.
He tries to make his voice sound farther and farther away.

I'll just be going, then.
Good luck with everything.
Goodbye, Genevieve!

He sticks his head into one side of the confessional.

SURPRISE!

>GENEVIEVE *sticks her head out the other side of the confessional.*

GENEVIEVE: I'm over here.

>*ST. PANCRAS turns around.*

ST. PANCRAS: Woof!

>GENEVIEVE *is startled by the mask.*

>ST. PANCRAS *is startled by* GENEVIEVE's *reaction.*

GENEVIEVE & ST. PANCRAS: AAAAH!

GENEVIEVE: What are you doing?

ST. PANCRAS: I'm trying to cheer you up.

GENEVIEVE: It isn't working.

ST. PANCRAS: *(taking off the mask)* Well, pardon me for trying.

GENEVIEVE: You're pardoned.

ST. PANCRAS: That's not what I meant.

>GENEVIEVE *goes back into her side of the confessional.*

Oh, don't be like that!

>GENEVIEVE *does not reply.* ST. PANCRAS *looks at the mask.*

There was a dog saint, you know. Well, not a real saint. But people worshipped him as if he was a saint. They cut his head off, too.

No reply.

Don't you think that's interesting?

No reply.

I think it's interesting. I'm not leaving.

Beat.

Oh, fine.

> ST. PANCRAS *enters the other side of the confessional. We are able to see inside it, as before. They both sit silently. Eventually, ST. PANCRAS starts to hum.*

GENEVIEVE: Do you mind?

ST. PANCRAS: Do I mind what?

GENEVIEVE: I want you to leave me alone.

ST. PANCRAS: Well, that's nonsense. You're never alone in a church. Why would you want to be alone?

GENEVIEVE: Why wouldn't I?

ST. PANCRAS: Would you like to talk about it?

GENEVIEVE: Did you talk to Him about my request?

ST. PANCRAS: . . . Who?

GENEVIEVE: You said you'd—

ST. PANCRAS: Not today, maybe tomorrow.

GENEVIEVE: You sound like my dad.

ST. PANCRAS: That's not very nice.

GENEVIEVE: You do.

ST. PANCRAS: There's no need to be rude.

GENEVIEVE: I'm not!

We hear footsteps approaching, the sound of coughing.

ST. PANCRAS: Do you hear that?

GENEVIEVE: Who is it?

FATHER enters. He genuflects to the altar, then stands looking out at it.

ST. PANCRAS: How should I know?

GENEVIEVE: Is it Father Paul?

ST. PANCRAS: Just a second.

ST. PANCRAS peeks out of his side of the confessional.

GENEVIEVE: Well?

ST. PANCRAS: It's your father.

GENEVIEVE: What?

ST. PANCRAS: *(louder)* Your father's out there.

GENEVIEVE: SSSSHHHH! What's he doing?

ST. PANCRAS: Let's see.

> *He peeks out his side of the confessional again.*

He isn't doing anything.

GENEVIEVE: He isn't coming to make another confession, is he?

ST. PANCRAS: I don't think so.

> *FATHER sits down in one of the pews. ST. PANCRAS peeks out and sees this.*

He's sitting down.

GENEVIEVE: Oh.

> *FATHER kneels.*

ST. PANCRAS: I think he's praying.

GENEVIEVE: About what?

ST. PANCRAS: I can't tell you that!

GENEVIEVE: Why not?

ST. PANCRAS: It's private!

GENEVIEVE: But—

ST. PANCRAS: Private!

GENEVIEVE: Fine.

ST. PANCRAS: Although . . .

GENEVIEVE: What?

ST. PANCRAS: Maybe we can provide a little divine intervention.

GENEVIEVE: What does that mean?

ST. PANCRAS: I mean maybe you can answer his prayers.

GENEVIEVE: How?

ST. PANCRAS: Talk to him.

GENEVIEVE: No!

ST. PANCRAS: I can disguise your voice. He'll never know it's you!

GENEVIEVE: But what if—

ST. PANCRAS: Are you saying you don't believe I can do it?

GENEVIEVE: No, but—

ST. PANCRAS: Say something!

GENEVIEVE: Like what?

ST. PANCRAS: Whatever comes into your head!

GENEVIEVE: Uhhh . . .

When they are speaking as the disembodied voice of the Lord, they miraculously speak in perfect unison. It's not clear which one of them is the brains behind the voice.

GENEVIEVE & ST. PANCRAS: DOMINUS VOBISCUM!

FATHER turns around. Beat. He turns back to face forward.

I'M TALKING TO YOU!

FATHER: . . . Hello?

GENEVIEVE & ST. PANCRAS: SILENCE!

FATHER: Who is that?

GENEVIEVE & ST. PANCRAS: I SAID SILENCE!

IN THE NAME OF THE LORD, WHO IS ME . . . I COMMAND THEE . . . THOU MUST . . . TELLETH THE TRUTH ABOUT MOM . . . I MEAN MARIE . . . TELLETH THE TRUTH TO THINE PRECIOUS DAUGHTER!

FATHER stands up and walks toward the confessional.

The interior of the confessional becomes invisible again.

GENEVIEVE: FURTHERMORE, THOU MUST—

He opens the door/pulls back the curtain. GENEVIEVE is alone.

FATHER: Genevieve?

GENEVIEVE: . . . Oh. Hi.

FATHER: What are you doing here?

GENEVIEVE: Nothing.

FATHER: Get out of there before someone sees you.

She exits the confessional.

You shouldn't be playing around in there.

GENEVIEVE: I wasn't!

FATHER: It's disrespectful.

GENEVIEVE: You don't even know what I was doing.

FATHER: What would Father Paul think if he saw you?

GENEVIEVE: He'd probably say girls aren't allowed in there, either.

FATHER: Genevieve. Sit down.

GENEVIEVE reluctantly sits in one of the pews.

Why aren't you in school?

GENEVIEVE: Why aren't you at work?

FATHER: Answer me.

GENEVIEVE: I had the afternoon off.

FATHER: Is that true?

GENEVIEVE: Why aren't you at work?

FATHER: Is it?

GENEVIEVE: . . . No.

FATHER: So you skipped school.

GENEVIEVE: Have you talked to Mom today?

FATHER: Don't change the subject--

GENEVIEVE: Have you?

FATHER: No, not today—

GENEVIEVE: *(sarcastically)* Oh, maybe tomorrow?

FATHER: Genevieve, that's enough—

GENEVIEVE: Do you ever tell the truth about anything? Where is she?

FATHER: Be quiet! What is the matter with you?

GENEVIEVE: Nothing.

FATHER: You're skipping school, you're being disrespectful to me, to Father Paul, to the Church—

GENEVIEVE: I heard you.

FATHER: What are you talking about?

GENEVIEVE: I heard you. In the confessional. Talking about Mom.

FATHER: You were listening in on my confession?

GENEVIEVE: It was an accident—

FATHER: That is private! It's my private business!

GENEVIEVE: I told you, I didn't mean to!

FATHER: You need to apologize—

GENEVIEVE: No!

FATHER: What?

GENEVIEVE: You're the one who should be sorry!

FATHER: Genevieve, lower your voice—

GENEVIEVE: Were you ever going to tell us?

FATHER: We are not discussing this here.

GENEVIEVE: Why not?

FATHER: Because it's none of your business! It's not anyone's business!

GENEVIEVE: It is my business! Why would you tell Father Paul what was going on and not me?

FATHER: I was telling God—

GENEVIEVE: Why would you bother telling him?

FATHER: What are you talking about?

GENEVIEVE: God already knows where she is!

FATHER: Genevieve—

GENEVIEVE: He knows where everyone is! He just doesn't want to tell us.

FATHER: That's not true—

GENEVIEVE: Why would He let her go missing? Why wouldn't He tell her to come back?

FATHER: I don't know.

GENEVIEVE: Or Martin?

FATHER: I don't know.

GENEVIEVE: Why would he do that?

FATHER: . . .

GENEVIEVE: It's not fair.

FATHER: No. It isn't.

GENEVIEVE: And you're not even trying to find her because you're too busy feeling sorry for yourself!

FATHER: I'm doing the best I can—

GENEVIEVE: No, you're not!

FATHER: You have no idea—

GENEVIEVE: You only got married because of Nicholas! She didn't even want to marry you!

FATHER: Genevieve—

GENEVIEVE: You probably didn't even want to have kids—

FATHER: Listen—

GENEVIEVE: Because you knew how terrible you'd be at it.

FATHER: Genevieve—

GENEVIEVE: I don't blame her for wanting to go somewhere else. I'll bet she marries someone a whole lot better and is a whole lot happier—

FATHER: The situation with your mother is between her and me—

GENEVIEVE: I'll bet she never even talks to any of us again, that's how unhappy you made her—

FATHER: We will deal with it when she's ready—

GENEVIEVE: *(loudly)* DEAR GOD—

FATHER: Genevieve!

GENEVIEVE: DEAR GOD, JUST SO YOU KNOW, I HOPE SHE NEVER COMES HOME IF SHE'S HAPPIER SOMEWHERE ELSE—

FATHER: Be quiet!

GENEVIEVE: EVEN THOUGH YOU'RE NOT LISTENING—

FATHER: We are going home!

> *FATHER tries to catch* GENEVIEVE *and put her coat on her, but she successfully evades him.*

GENEVIEVE: BECAUSE YOU PROBABLY DON'T CARE—OR MAYBE YOU DON'T EVEN EXIST.

FATHER: GENEVIEVE!

GENEVIEVE: You don't even EXIST! AMEN! AMEN AMEN AMEN!

FATHER: *(shouting)* Genevieve. Stop it. STOP IT, YOU'RE RIGHT!

GENEVIEVE *stops running around.*

You're right. I should have told you sooner. I don't know why this is happening. I don't know why any of these things happened. I should have told you and your brothers. But I don't know how to . . . I don't know what I should have done. I know you're upset. But you can't make a scene here, no matter how angry you are. If you want to have a tantrum, you can go to your room when we get home. Now get your things.

GENEVIEVE: No.

FATHER: Get your things, Genevieve.

GENEVIEVE: It's not fair.

FATHER: Life isn't fair.

GENEVIEVE: I'm calling Grandma when I get home. Maybe she can help us. Or at least she'll want to talk about it.

FATHER: . . .

GENEVIEVE: Who cares what she thinks of you?

FATHER: Come on.

GENEVIEVE: Maybe I should call her now. Maybe Father Paul will let me use his phone.

FATHER: Maybe Father Paul would be interested to hear about you eavesdropping on peoples' confessions.

GENEVIEVE: Should we go talk to him together?

Beat.

I'm not coming with you.

FATHER: I'll be in the car. Be out in ten minutes.

GENEVIEVE'S FATHER exits. She looks up.

GENEVIEVE: What?

Beat. There is no response.

I'm sorry for yelling.

Beat.

And for saying you don't exist.

What do you care, anyway? I know, you don't. Or you can't see me.

But you could try. Just look down. Just look down for once.

Please?

Can St. Pancras come back?

A sound from inside the confessional. She goes toward it.

St. Pancras?

No answer. She walks toward ST. PANCRAS's *side of the confessional.*

Hello?

She opens the door/pulls back the curtain of his side. It is empty.

Oh.

MARTIN bursts out from the other side of the confessional. He carries his hockey stick, playing an imaginary game like the first time we met him. He wears the dog mask pulled up on top of his head, like a goalie's mask. His face is even more decomposed than the last time we saw him.

Oh!

MARTIN: He blows past the defence . . . he's a one-man power play! The rest of his team has stopped to watch him! The other team has stopped to watch him! He's taking it to the net! He shoots . . . HE SCORES! Ladies and gentlemen, the other team is leaving the ice, they are giving up, they—

He notices GENEVIEVE.

Oh, hi.

GENEVIEVE: How long have you been in there?

MARTIN: Where?

He holds up his hockey stick.

I found it.

GENEVIEVE: Good for you.

MARTIN: I thought it was gone forever. Oh! Look what else I found!

> *He pulls the dog mask down over his face and runs around* GENEVIEVE *a few times, doing some fancy stick work.*

(referring to the mask) Can I have this?

GENEVIEVE: Sure.

MARTIN: Thanks.

> *He pulls the mask back up.*

What are you doing here?

GENEVIEVE: It's a long story.

MARTIN: Weirdo.

GENEVIEVE: Don't.

MARTIN: Why are you so grouchy?

GENEVIEVE: I'm not.

MARTIN: Uh-huh. Did you talk to Father Paul yet?

GENEVIEVE: There's no point.

MARTIN: Have you been practising?

GENEVIEVE: Practising what?

MARTIN: The bells, dummy.

GENEVIEVE: He's never going to let me do it.

MARTIN: We should practise right now.

GENEVIEVE: What? Here?

MARTIN: Yes, here.

GENEVIEVE: I don't think that's—

MARTIN: How are you going to replace me if you don't practise?

GENEVIEVE: I—

MARTIN: Maybe you'll even get to serve at my funeral. They'll let you out of school.

GENEVIEVE: They'll probably let everybody out of school.

MARTIN: Really?

GENEVIEVE: Probably.

MARTIN: Wow.

GENEVIEVE: Martin—

MARTIN: The important thing is not to stare at the coffin.

GENEVIEVE: Why?

MARTIN: Father Paul says it's rude.

GENEVIEVE: It probably reminds people there's someone in there.

MARTIN: I guess.

GENEVIEVE: If there's someone in there.

MARTIN: What does that mean?

GENEVIEVE: Nothing.

MARTIN: Are you ready?

GENEVIEVE: I guess.

MARTIN: Get the bells.

GENEVIEVE: I can't—

MARTIN: Behind you.

The bells are indeed behind her. GENEVIEVE *goes to get them.*

GENEVIEVE: Here.

MARTIN: Put them down. Quietly.

She does.

MARTIN: In nomine Patris et Filii et Spiritus Sanctus.

GENEVIEVE: What are you doing?

MARTIN: Get ready.

He goes to the altar.

GENEVIEVE: We can't go up there!

MARTIN: Why not?

GENEVIEVE: This isn't a mass.

MARTIN: Father Paul told me that the priest is always praying for the altar servers in particular.

GENEVIEVE: So?

MARTIN: So I'm praying for you.

GENEVIEVE: Can I just ring the bells?

MARTIN: Not yet.

GENEVIEVE: For practise?

MARTIN: No. You have to wait till the priest stretches his arms forward over the chalice.

GENEVIEVE: Okay.

MARTIN: So wait.

  MARTIN is praying.

GENEVIEVE: Well? Are you going to do it?

MARTIN: I'm not finished yet.

GENEVIEVE: Martin—

  MARTIN stretches his hands over the chalice as if he's casting a spell.

MARTIN: OKAY, RING IT NOW!

> GENEVIEVE *rings the bell.*

STOP!

> GENEVIEVE *stops.*

The Consecration.

> MARTIN *produces a sandwich from one of his pockets. It stands in for the host.* GENEVIEVE *takes the bells and kneels behind* MARTIN, *slightly to his right.*

> MARTIN *says the text of the Consecration to himself. He genuflects.* GENEVIEVE *bows deeply, rings the bell, and kneels upright again.*

> MARTIN *"elevates" the sacred sandwich.*

Now lift the chasuble.

GENEVIEVE: You're not wearing one.

MARTIN: Pretend.

> GENEVIEVE *lifts the lower edge of* MARTIN's *Habs jersey.*

> *She rings the bell when* MARTIN *says "My Lord and my God," and releases the jersey as* MARTIN *lowers his hands.*

> *When* MARTIN *kneels again, she bows deeply, gives the bell one ring, and kneels upright again while* MARTIN *holds the sandwich high.*

> *While* MARTIN *says the Latin, she translates.*

MARTIN: Qui pridie quam pateretur, accepit panem in sanctas ac venerabiles manus suas et elevatis oculis in caelum ad te Deum Patrem suum omnipotentem, tibi gratias agens, benedixit, fregit, deditique discipulis suis, dicens:

Accipte, et manducate ex hoc omnes,
Hoc est enim corpus meum.

GENEVIEVE: The day before He suffered, He took bread into His holy and venerable hands, and with His eyes raised to Heaven, unto Thee, God, His almighty Father, giving thanks to Thee, He blessed it, broke it, and gave it to His disciples saying:

Take all of you, and eat of this:
For this is my body.

MARTIN freezes.

GENEVIEVE: What is it?

MARTIN: It's the wine now.

GENEVIEVE: Right.

MARTIN: I think we should skip that part.

GENEVIEVE: Why?

MARTIN: It makes me nervous.

GENEVIEVE: Oh. Martin—

MARTIN: Let's skip it.

GENEVIEVE: Fine, we'll skip it.

MARTIN: Okay, so then the wine, and then Haec quotiescum que feceritis, in mei memoriam facietis.

GENEVIEVE: As often as you do these things, you do them in memory of Me.

She rings the bell. Beat.

MARTIN *becomes an altar server again and does these movements along with* GENEVIEVE.

MARTIN: Take the bell, get up, turn left, come down the steps, genuflect, turn right, kneel at your old spot. Put the bell down quietly.

GENEVIEVE: Okay.

MARTIN: QUIETLY.

GENEVIEVE: I am. Now what.

MARTIN: The absolution of the dead.

GENEVIEVE: Martin—

MARTIN: At funeral masses only.

GENEVIEVE: Why do they need to be absolved? They're dead.

MARTIN: Absolve, quaesumus Domine, animam famuli tui— To Thou, we pray, O Lord, deliver the soul of Thy servant—and then you say their name— Say it.

GENEVIEVE: Martin.

MARTIN: Ab omni vinculo delictorum: ut in resurrectionis gloria inter Sanctor et electos tuos resuscitatus respiret. Per Dominum nostrum Jesum Christum Filium tuum, qui tecum vivit et regnat in unitate Spiritus Sancti Deus—

GENEVIEVE: From every bond of guilt, that in the glory of the resurrection, He may live again, raised up to the fellowship of Thy saints and the elect. Through Our Lord Jesus Christ, Thy Son, Who being God, live and reigns with Thee in the unity of the Holy Ghost—

MARTIN: Per omnia saecula saeculorum.

GENEVIEVE: For ever and ever.

MARTIN: Amen.

GENEVIEVE: Amen.

MARTIN: Dominus vobiscum.

GENEVIEVE: And also with you.

MARTIN: Requiescant in pace.

GENEVIEVE: May they rest in peace.

> *Beat.*

And then what happens?

MARTIN: Then they go to the cemetery.

GENEVIEVE: What happens there?

MARTIN: I don't know.

GENEVIEVE: Oh.

MARTIN: I always go downstairs to get something to eat. Genevieve, I always went downstairs instead.

GENEVIEVE: I'm sure it isn't anything bad—

MARTIN: How do you know? You've never even been to a funeral.

GENEVIEVE: Well, no, but—

MARTIN: Oh. I should have gone. I should have gone just once, to see what happens.

GENEVIEVE: Maybe I can go with you.

MARTIN: I don't think you can.

GENEVIEVE: Girls can do anything—

MARTIN: I think I have to do this part by myself.

GENEVIEVE: Well, do you have to do it right now? I don't think Father Paul would mind if you waited downstairs for a while.

MARTIN: Do you think I'll forget?

GENEVIEVE: Forget what?

MARTIN: Everything. Who I am. That I even existed.

GENEVIEVE: You won't.

MARTIN: How do you know?

GENEVIEVE: Oh.

MARTIN: What if I forget?

GENEVIEVE: Well, I won't. Forget.

MARTIN: Promise?

GENEVIEVE: I promise. And if you think you might be forgetting, just look down.

MARTIN: From where?

GENEVIEVE: From wherever you end up. Look down. I'm easy to find. I don't think I'm going anywhere.

MARTIN: That's what I thought.

GENEVIEVE: Well. I . . . I'm sorry, Martin.

MARTIN: Don't worry about it.

GENEVIEVE: Promise to look? Once in a while?

MARTIN: Sure.

GENEVIEVE: Promise.

MARTIN: Okay, fine, I promise.

> *Beat.*

I guess . . . I guess I should go.

GENEVIEVE: Okay.

MARTIN: Okay.

Beat.

GENEVIEVE: See you later?

MARTIN: Not if I see you first.

GENEVIEVE: Good one.

> MARTIN *exits into the confessional. After a moment,* GENEVIEVE *goes and opens the door/curtain. No one is there.*
>
> *She looks around, gathers up her things, and exits.*
>
> *Later, in* GENEVIEVE'*s bedroom. She's reading a textbook/magazine/something about space.*

The Soviet Union launched *Sputnik* on October 4, 1957. It took about ninety-six minutes to circle the Earth. People could even watch it pass by in the sky overhead and hear its beeping over the radio. *Sputnik* fell from orbit and burned up in the atmosphere on—

> *There is a knock at her bedroom door. She looks up but does not respond, continues reading. Another knock.*

FATHER: Genevieve?

GENEVIEVE: What.

FATHER: It's suppertime.

GENEVIEVE: I'm not hungry.

FATHER: Can I come in?

GENEVIEVE: No.

FATHER: I have something for you.

GENEVIEVE: Fine.

He comes in holding an envelope.

What do you want?

FATHER: This came for you today.

He holds out an envelope. She takes it.

GENEVIEVE: What is it?

FATHER: I think it's from Mom.

GENEVIEVE examines the letter. It's still sealed.

I didn't open it.

GENEVIEVE: Why not?

FATHER: It's addressed to you.

GENEVIEVE: Oh. Thanks.

Beat.

FATHER: I'll leave you alone.

GENEVIEVE: You can wait here. If you want.

FATHER: I'll go downstairs. Dinner's almost ready.

GENEVIEVE: Okay.

> *He exits.* GENEVIEVE *stares at the letter for a while. She opens it and reads:*

Dear Genevieve,

I'm sorry I've been away so long without calling or writing. I'm sure you must be angry with me. I had to go away and think about some things alone. That might sound selfish. I'd tell you you'll understand when you're older, but I know how much you hate that. I'd tell you that life is never simple, but I think you know that already.

Your father and I have some things to work out, but I don't want you to worry about that. Please keep reading and going to school and asking questions that annoy people. Keep being yourself no matter what anyone else says. I know that you have a beautiful purpose waiting to be discovered.

It may be a while till I can come and see you, but I will be thinking of you every day until then. If you ever feel sad or alone, close your eyes and think of me, and know that I'm thinking about you too. Maybe we can have Christmas at Grandma's, just like when you were little.

Until then, all my love,

Mom

> *There is a faint sound of bells coming from somewhere close by.*
>
> GENEVIEVE *stops and looks around. The bells ring again.*
>
> *She rushes to the closet and opens the door.*
>
> *The closet is empty. She waits, but the bells do not ring again.*

She closes the closet door, then kneels as in the first scene.

Heavenly Father . . .

She stops.

St. Pancras . . .

She stops again.

Dear St. Martin,
I found her. Well, sort of. But at least she's alive. No offence.
I hope your parents find you.

Do you see me?

She waves.

I hope you can see me.
It's nice to have someone looking out for you, even if they can be kind
of a jerk sometimes.

Just kidding.

Anyway, please bless all the space dogs and saint dogs and all the regular
dogs too. And Father Paul and all the altar servers. And please, please
look out for my mother and brothers. And especially my father. But
don't tell him I told you to, because it's probably a sin to pray to you, and
I'm not going to mention it in my confession, so don't even—I'm sorry.

Please tell St. Pancras not to be too unhappy. Maybe you can show him
how to play hockey.

Do you think you could appear to Father Paul? Just to give him a little
nudge?

Can you hear me?
Can you?

> *Beat.*

On second thought, don't tell me.
Amen.

> *Blackout. In the darkness, the faint beeping of a satellite.*

> *End of play.*

Acknowledgements

Do This In Memory of Me was written with the financial support of the Edmonton Arts Council, and received workshop support through the 2016 Citadel Theatre Playwrights Forum.

Originally from Ottawa, Cat Walsh is an award-winning performer and playwright based in Edmonton, Alberta. Her plays include the site-specific *Anxiety* (Theatre Yes), the gas-station gothic *The Laws of Thermodynamics* (Theatre Yes/Workshop West Playwrights' Theatre), solo thriller *eleven-oh-four* (charm/strange theatre), and the quantum-inspired *Fetch* (Interloper Theatre). Cat is a graduate of the University of Ottawa.

First edition: October 2021
Printed and bound in Canada by Imprimerie Gauvin, Gatineau

Jacket design by Kisscut Design
Cover image © Goce Ilievski/Stocksy.com
Author photo © Ryan Parker

PLAYWRIGHTS
CANADA PRESS

202-269 Richmond St. W.
Toronto, ON
M5V 1X1

416.703.0013
info@playwrightscanada.com
www.playwrightscanada.com
@playcanpress

MIX
Paper from
responsible sources
FSC® C100212